PENGUIN ENTERPRISE
THE MANUAL FOR INDIAN START-UPS

VIJAYA KUMAR IVATURI (or IVK, as he is better known) is the co-founder and CTO of Crayon Data, a big data analytics products company based in Singapore, with a development centre in Chennai. He has been associated with the ICT industry for over thirty years, and is one of the leading experts in innovation management and advanced technologies incubation in India.

MEENA GANESH founded and led, or co-promoted, some of India's most disruptive start-ups, including Portea Medical, CustomerAsset, TutorVista, BigBasket, Bluestone, FreshMenu, AcadGild, Avagmah, among others. A part of the board of governors of IIM Calcutta, she also serves on CII's councils for innovation and entrepreneurship, and healthcare.

ALOK MITTAL is co-founder and CEO of Indifi, a platform for enabling debt financing for small businesses. Alok is also an active angel investor, co-founder of Indian Angel Network, and on the board of TiE (The Indus Entrepreneurs) Delhi. Prior to establishing Indifi, he set up and ran Canaan Partners' operations in India, investing in high-growth technology and Internet start-ups.

SRIRAM SUBRAMANYA founded Integra Software Services, a content solutions company servicing global education publishers. What started off as a five-member team twenty-five years ago today is a 2000 people organisation with offices in four countries, positioning Integra as one of the top-ten digital content services companies for publishers worldwide.

PROFESSOR SADAGOPAN is the director of IIIT-Bangalore. After obtaining his PhD from Purdue University (USA), he taught at IIT Kanpur and IIM Bangalore. He is widely travelled, has written extensively on all aspects of IT, consulted for industry, served on corporate boards and helped start-ups for more than two decades.

The additional contributors for the chapters and templates include Dr Aravind Chinchure, Symbiosis International University; Priamvada Princeton, K-Law; Kavita Chowkimane, Portea Medical; and Aarti Ramakrishnan, Crayon Data.

PRAISE FOR THE BOOK

'This book could not have come at a better time than now, when we are witnessing bold young Indians venturing out on their own, disrupting industries and creating new opportunities. This step-by-step start-up guide, written by first-generation entrepreneurs (who have been there and done that) and a professor, is a must-read for the new set of trailblazers.'

C.K. RANGANATHAN, FOUNDER-CHAIRMAN, CAVINKARE

'Great to see a book tailored specifically for the Indian start-up ecosystem which goes beyond the "rags to riches" or "ra-ra" narrative. With the average age of first-time entrepreneurs entering the start-up ecosystem going down steadily, this book is a must-read for all those embarking on the journey. It will serve as a good primer and provide help across many areas from mentors, advisers and professionals. The contents of the book will help entrepreneurs to reflect on and structure their thinking. It is good to see first-time authors and practising entrepreneurs writing the book—it makes it a lot more credible and much less academic. Hope more such books are birthed in India.'

K. GANESH, CHAIRMAN, PORTEA MEDICAL, AND SERIAL ENTREPRENEUR

VIJAYA KUMAR IVATURI, MEENA GANESH,
ALOK MITTAL, SRIRAM SUBRAMANYA
AND PROF. SADAGOPAN

The
Manual
for
Indian
Start-ups

TOOLS TO START AND SCALE-UP
YOUR NEW VENTURE

PENGUIN
ENTERPRISE

An imprint of Penguin Random House

PENGUIN ENTERPRISE

USA | Canada | UK | Ireland | Australia
New Zealand | India | South Africa | China | Singapore

Penguin Enterprise is part of the Penguin Random House group of companies
whose addresses can be found at global.penguinrandomhouse.com

Published by Penguin Random House India Pvt. Ltd
4th Floor, Capital Tower 1, MG Road,
Gurugram 122 002, Haryana, India

Penguin
Random House
India

First published in Penguin Enterprise by Penguin Random House India 2017
Penguin Enterprise is the custom-publishing imprint of Penguin Random House India

ISBN 9780143450856

Typeset in Adobe Garamond Pro by Sahadat Ali

Printed at Manipal Technologies Limited, India

www.penguin.co.in

For start-up entrepreneurs everywhere: those who dream big and take the plunge!

CONTENTS

ACKNOWLEDGEMENTS

We would like to express our sincere gratitude to Ram Narayan, VP, Technology and Managing Site Director at VMware; Venkat Raju, CEO, PVTM Solutions; Ganesh Jayadevan, VP and Head of India Operations, Jifflenow, for their content contributions on the topic of product management.

We thank Raj Ramachandran and Sindhu Nayak of JSA, a leading law firm in India, and Shipra Paul of Crayon Data, for their contribution and valuable inputs on the topics of data privacy and POSH (Prevention of Sexual Harassment).

We thank Dipti Nair of Your Story for providing the contacts and case studies from the MSME sector in India. We thank Akash of Rageonline, Amit Jain of Shingora Textiles & Zenscale and Rishi Pahwa of Avon Cycles, for sharing their learnings on growing businesses in India.

We thank Priyanka Mukhija and Vignesh Kumar of CII for helping us with the list of incubators in India as well as for the introductions to the MSME players in India for gathering inputs from them.

Our sincere thanks to C.A. Pavan of BCL India for providing key inputs on GST-related matters.

Finally, we express our deep gratitude to Kris Gopalakrishnan for his continuous support and encouragement for helping evolve this book to reflect the latest topics of interest for start-ups. We take this opportunity to thank Vikram Kirloskar, president, CII, for his support for the content development for this book under National Startup Council of CII, which is the framework under which this work was undertaken.

We thank Akhilesh Soodan and Ankita Poddar at Penguin for their excellent support to get this second edition through.

FOREWORD

Kris Gopalakrishnan

When I had led the discussions as the Chairman of the CII Start-up Council on the need for an India-specific start-up manual in 2015, I never imagined that the manual would be such a stupendous success, with more than 8,000 copies sold, and that I would be writing a foreword for the second edition. It is very gratifying to know that the book received such a degree of acceptance and appreciation for its content and addressed an important content gap in the Indian start-up ecosystem.

The start-up ecosystem has evolved significantly from 2015, and there are many changes across various functional areas that have become more relevant as Indian start-ups have scaled and matured in both content and operational models. The publication of the first edition and its wider audience reach across India provided us with some deep insights about what the gaps are and where the greatest need was felt in terms of a focus for the second edition.

The growing domestic market for Indian start-ups gave rise to a much more formal structuring of product management as a function. As there is very little information available on the topic in the local ecosystem, everyone started leveraging from product management experiences in the west.

The introduction of GST changed the regulatory and compliance landscape for start-ups in India. The growing importance of data privacy and GDPR reference is pushing many start-ups and MSMEs to put the necessary processes in place for assurance and compliance in this area. The shift to manufacturing in India has opened up new opportunities for many start-ups and MSMEs to add value to the supply chain for the local manufacturing of goods. There are little or no insights available for such firms in terms of global practices regarding data, people and processes.

As women become a major contributor to workforce productivity in India, it is becoming more relevant to put a framework in place for start-ups and MSME sectors for managing a mixed gender workforce. The Act for prevention of sexual harassment at the workplace (POSH) is a measure that provides guidelines for establishing such a framework even in smaller organizations like MSMEs and start-ups. As they do not have full-fledged and mature HR functions, it is important to provide some inputs and insights to the smaller firms on what POSH is and what it is not.

Given the number of changes that have taken place in the recent years, I thought that there is a need for a new edition of the manual and picked up the topic in last year's council meetings. Based on the deliberations we had in the start-up council, I asked the authors to come up with a new edition covering the topics mentioned above, and with the contents refreshed to suit the present times.

The second edition captures these topics in a lucid manner and provides some practical advice on what to act upon. It shares some real-world experiences in the Indian context. The second edition preserves the manual and narrative styles of the first, but contains updated and additional information for a start-up or MSME to refer to and implement.

I thank all the authors and the other contributors for their efforts and wish them all the best for this second edition.

FOREWORD

Vikram Kirloskar

This manual has been a very helpful and informative handbook for Indian start-ups developing disruptive products and business models while trying to flourish in the unique Indian entrepreneurial ecosystem. This is an excellent publication addressing several critical aspects for Indian start-ups—namely, ideation, team formation, registration, compliance requirements, IPR, marketing, funding and management of human resources.

It is heartening to note that the second edition of the manual is getting published within a short span of two years since the book's first appearance. It only goes to show how the book has been accepted and appreciated by its target audience, the Indian start-up. In its second edition, the book's coverage expands to include certain new developments, such as compliance with GST, data privacy and something of more serious nature—prevention of sexual harassment in workplaces.

I am sure that the book in its present form will serve as an armoury of knowledge for Indian start-ups and help entrepreneurs with what they need to know before jumping into a venture.

AUTHORS' NOTE

When we had published the book two years ago, we had never anticipated the stupendous success it would achieve. The first edition book sold more than 8,000 copies in two years, and that is a very good record for first-time authors and for the only book of its kind in India.

We had received very positive response to the book and some valuable suggestions as well for coverage of new topics going forward. This second edition is an attempt to cover some of the most important topics that have become relevant in recent times because of changes in the regulations as well as the maturing of the start-up ecosystem in India.

Given the rise of product start-ups in India, there is a need felt in the ecosystem for a primer on the topic of product management, with the addition of some India-specific experiences in the Indian context. There is also an introduction of GST, GDPR & data privacy compliance for ventures. There was an express need for covering these topics in a manual of this nature. With the rise in the number of start-ups in India in both depth and breadth of coverage, there are many people-related matters which are emerging as important factors for management attention as well as compliance requirements. POSH (Prevention of Sexual Harassment at the Workplace) is an important issue for new-age start-ups now and a dimension that cannot be ignored in a young and diversified workforce.

We have added product management, data privacy covering GDPR and POSH as additional chapters in this second edition. We have included some perspectives on these topics in terms of actual case studies or real-world experiences to illustrate both India-specific situations and popular global practices.

We have revised the list of incubators and a few checklists to include new requirements like GST, and have updated the reference material too.

We hope you will enjoy reading the second edition as much as we did in writing it.

ACKNOWLEDGEMENTS

(First edition)

A book of this nature cannot be written without the express support of many people in the industry and academia. We have learnt a lot from many sources, got inspired by many stories and immensely benefited from many other contributors.

While it is not possible to thank all those people who helped us with a particular list, in a limited space like this, there are, however, a few individuals whom we want to thank for their explicit contribution and support.

Kris Gopalakrishnan for inspiring us to work on this project and nudging us to think big and publish the work as a book. We would not have embarked on this without his encouragement.

Anjan Das, Jibak Dasgupta and Gaurav Gupta of CII for setting up the first forum for the authors to collaborate as a part of the CII national task force in the form of a start-up council. It was CII's introduction to Penguin that kick-started this project as a book-publication effort based on the council's foundation work on this topic.

We thank Deep Kalra of MakeMyTrip; C.K. Ranganathan of CavinKare; K. Ganesh of Portea Medical and GrowthStory; Naushad Forbes, chairman of CII; and Chandrajit Banerjee, director general of CII, for taking time out of their busy schedules and reviewing the text. Their insightful comments and generous praise for the book is a tribute to all those who helped us to put this work together for the start-up system in India.

We appreciate the time and effort taken by the promoters of the firms in sharing their valuable experience with the readers here, and we would like to thank K. Ganesh of Portea Medical; Aishwarya Singh of JustRide; Srikanth Iyer of HomeLane; Anjali Schiavina of Mandala Apparels; Amarnath Krishnamurthy of SG industries; Mrigank Tripathi of Qustn Technologies; Ganapathy of Axilor Ventures; Komal Preet of Placitum IP; Nikesh Garera of EventsHigh; Ashish Nichani and Sudarsan Metla of Place of Origin; and Abir Barua of Crayon Data.

Our sincere thanks to the following contributors who created the narrative sections for the specific topics we requested for and spent time with us in evolving them to suit the book's focus and style: Aarti Ramakrishnan of Crayon Data; Kavita Chowkimane of Portea Medical; Dr Aravind Chinchure of Symbiosis International University; Ganapathy Venugopal and Payal Shah of Axilor Ventures; Lalit Ahuja and Venkat Raju of Kyron Accelerator; Priamvada Princeton, Abhishek, Prateek Mohapatra, Shria Soundararajan, Keertan Sreekumar, Siri H.S. of K-Law; and Samuel Mani of Mani Chengappa & Mathur (MCM), a Bangalore-based law firm.

We would like to thank the following people for helping us with their views, contacts and relevant information, which contributed to building narratives for the different chapters in the book: Ramesh Sundararaman of IIIT-B; Dr Joseph George of Workplace Catalysts; author and economics historian Shankar Jaganathan; Mridula Pai of Crayon Data; and Vishal Krishna of YourStory.

Being first-time authors ourselves (with the exception of Prof. Sadagopan), we needed a lot of handholding and education on how to write and publish a book with the readers' view in context rather than the authors' expert views on the subject. In this regard, our heartfelt thanks to the entire team at Penguin, including Rakesh Chander, Rachita Raj, Akhilesh Soodan and Sameer Mahale. We thank Kripa Raman, our business editor; Ateendriya Gupta, our copy editor, and illustrator Gautam Koushik. Our special thanks again to Rachita Raj for putting up with our iterations and delivering on impossible deadlines for printing.

Our first book-writing journey would not have been possible without a stellar support system at home, and we express our gratitude to our respective families for putting up with our ever-changing schedules, mood swings and our requests for quick on-the-fly feedback from them. Thank you all for everything.

FOREWORD

Kris Gopalakrishnan
(First edition)

The genesis of the book *The Manual for Indian Start-ups* is rooted in my own conviction that India needs its own manual for start-ups, given its diversity in market segments, business models and consumer behaviour. Given my long corporate experience as one of the founders of Infosys, and my current interests and commitments in the Indian ecosystem through my own trusts and Axilor Ventures, I have learnt that we need to leverage proven global business models and emerging technologies for our early-stage ventures to succeed at scale. However, the operating models of start-up ventures in India differ from the Western models in terms of team composition and dynamics, funding models and customer-engagement models. There is a gap at the ground level for dimensions of engagement.

I had chaired a CII national council on innovation and entrepreneurship in 2015. Now called 'Start-up Council', one of the task forces worked on the toolkit needed for the early-stage promoters in India in their first three years of the journey. At the end of the task-force period, and based on the output produced by the group, I had asked them to publish it as a book and not limit the scope of the work itself to a report in CII. The group worked for the last one year to transform this start-up process manual into a proper publication in collaboration with Penguin Random House.

The manual is a handy paperback edition of nearly 200 pages, with key templates explained for seed funding, founders' agreement, employee agreement, mentor agreement, and so on, as well as some short narratives about the different phases and stages in a start-up and what the typical practices of the start-up ecosystem in India are.

The book's authors are well known and seasoned industry professionals and entrepreneurs themselves, and, therefore, the book is almost like a practitioner's manual. Vijaya Kumar Ivaturi (popularly known as IVK) is the lead author, and he is former CTO of Wipro and the current co-founder and CTO of Crayon Data. His co-authors are Meena Ganesh, CEO of Portea Medical and a serial entrepreneur; Alok Mittal, an angel investor, co-founder of IAN and the ex-head of Canaan Partners; Prof. Sadagopan, director of IIIT-Bangalore; and Sriram Subramanya, chairman and MD of Integra Software.

This is the first-of-its-kind manual for start-ups in India, and is the maiden book-writing venture for the authors as well! I wish them the very best for this endeavour.

Kris Gopalakrishnan
Chairman, Axilor Ventures
Co-founder, Infosys Ltd
Former chairman, CII

FOREWORD

Naushad Forbes

(First edition)

Established as the key industry body in India, the Confederation of Indian Industry, or CII (as it is best known) has nurtured the growth of industry for more than a century. As the voice of Indian industry, CII champions the cause of corporates and SMEs in the Indian ecosystem. Its origins in core engineering expanded early into manufacturing and services, but a focus on start-ups has been missing.

CII has long understood the importance of entrepreneurship as a driver of innovation and the economy more generally. This understanding translated into various initiatives over the years, which have been endorsed by the Government of India through many schemes. These external developments led CII to form a high-level 'Council on Start-ups' comprising key industry members and experts, under the leadership of Kris Gopalakrishnan, co-founder of Infosys and a past president of CII.

CII has also advocated a clear policy position to address the needs of start-ups. We believe that what start-ups most need is not concessions but a removal of the heavy hand of the state. In consultation with our Start-up Council, we have correspondingly advocated that a start-up be defined as any firm less than five years old, with no further qualification. All interaction with the state must then be entirely on the basis of self-declaration, with no need to get any permissions or approvals. We believe this can unleash entrepreneurship in the country to spawn millions of start-ups and many millions of good jobs in five years' time.

The CII Start-up Council has been instrumental in recognizing and implementing various initiatives to boost the start-up ecosystem. The major challenge in developing rural start-ups and entrepreneurs is a severe shortage of role models and access to mentors. The concept of a start-up cookbook was conceived by the CII Start-up Council, and a task force was formed to work on it.

The members of this task force, who authored this book, have put in a lot of effort over a year of multiple rounds of consultation, revisions and iterations. The book has evolved as a ready reference for the countless who wish to float a business venture in urban or rural areas. *The Manual for Indian Start-ups* offers an excellent compilation and explanation of templates and agreements, covering areas of seed funding, founders' agreements, employee engagement, mentor collaborations and others. The manual also includes short narratives about the different phases and stages of a start-up, and the outlines of the typical practices that start-ups follow within the Indian ecosystem.

I congratulate Kris, the Start-up Council and the authors of the book for producing such an essential work.

Naushad Forbes
Chairman, CII
Co-chairman, Forbes Marshall

AUTHORS' NOTE

(First edition)

CII Task Force: Paving the Way

As members of a CII national committee on innovation and entrepreneurship in 2015, we formed a task force to develop artefacts that could be used by the promoters of start-ups in India in the initial years of their entrepreneurial journey. The authors are the members of this task force and developed a recommendation in terms of advice, typical practices in Indian start-ups and a few guidelines for the key contracts needed in the early stages of the start-up journey.

Addressing the Gap in the Market vis-à-vis Appropriate Literature

The main driver for this was based on the observations made by many experts of the start-up ecosystem that there was hardly any India-specific literature available for the modern age's promoters to leverage beyond some inspirational stories covered in business books. One saw numerous international bestsellers at that time that dealt with early-stage venturing;

however, many of them needed to be tuned and adapted to the Indian scenario. There were many forums and templates but none of them carried a narrative, coupled with the context and logical flow that was needed to work for the new promoter.

Based on the task-force interim report submitted at the CII meeting chaired by Kris Gopalakrishnan, it was suggested that the recommendations be made into a full-fledged process manual for start-ups and be published as a book for general consumption. The task force led by Vijaya Kumar Ivaturi decided to take up the challenge of converting its report into a book in publishable format and formed a lead authors' team with the same members of the task force.

The Scope of the Book

It took a lot of effort to determine the scope of this book based on the work done by the task force—we had to find a balance between the coverage of topics and the volume of the book. We decided to limit the content to those critical topics that are relevant to the first three years of a typical start-up journey. The book is written in a sector-agnostic way, and the focus is on the common elements of work streams in a typical start-up in its early stages, independent of the domain it belongs to. Therefore, the depth element for a typical manufacturing start-up, a cloud-based Web business start-up or a services start-up has been kept out of the scope of this book, with emphasis being placed more on the functional aspects of the business.

The Format of the Book

We decided to follow a linear format in the book to ensure that a logical sequence is maintained to reflect things 'as they happen' in a start-up journey. However, it is not required to peruse the text in a linear fashion, and one can always go to the specific section of interest based on the phase a start-up is in.

Narrative versus Template

Our initial aim was to provide a set of key templates for promoters to read, understand and use by customizing them to their own context. Upon discovering that there is no book that provides templates, we picked the most important and common ones for the founders' agreement, employee agreement, adviser agreement and seed investor agreement. However, we do not intend to provide a form to fill in the details. These templates are built to explain the most important operative clauses in the aforementioned agreements and the typical practice in India for their real-world use. Though they capture the popular clauses for discussion, and their explanations thereof, promoters cannot do away with working alongside their lawyers to ensure that the templates are complete for their own use and relevance.

As we did not want to create a book of templates alone, we ended up writing a narrative about the different aspects of the early-stage journey, in the form of a primer, to explain, share and provide some insights as well. We have enlisted different people from diverse sectors to contribute to this work and have stitched the content together into one long linear flow.

Intended Readers of the Book

The templates were built in consultation with leading lawyers and we have added some comments and practices for their use to ensure real-world relevance. We have not kept a sector context in mind here and therefore they are indicative in nature. The intended audience for the book are people in the first to third years of their start-up journey.

Tried-and-tested Templates

The authors have used the templates provided in this book with many start-ups in order to gauge their relevance and utility in the context of the real world. We have found them to be extremely useful in providing a primer to several fresh, albeit inexperienced, promoters. They have also served as the baseline to debate with the other party and arrive on the specific terms and numbers before approaching a lawyer to draft them into contracts. In a nutshell, the templates provided here have been tested and were very well received—they provide a huge operational and conceptual value to a new promoter.

Our First Attempt

This is our first serious attempt to write a long-form book. With the exception of Prof. Sadagopan, none of us have any authorial experience and have learnt the ropes the hard way! It took us much more time than we expected, and perhaps even left us wondering, in certain moments, whether we would be able to complete the book as the scope kept increasing.

Sequel

We have made an explicit effort to ensure that the book is accessible and compact in size; to enable this we have had to omit several other templates and topics. We plan to address these either in the sequel to this book or in a future edition. To conclude, we are first-time authors, as mentioned earlier, learning the craft on the go, so do excuse any errors!

INTRODUCTION

a built-up view (and more) of what entrepreneurs must
be aware of and look out for, given all efforts up to an
entrepreneur's hub, and the best practitioners advance on
be worries without the pitfalls left.

INTRODUCTION

This manual covers the key elements of a typical start-up process and the start-up stages in an Indian scenario. It captures the basic principles, key practices and expert views to give fledgling Indian entrepreneurs a good preliminary guide to consult during any phase of their start-up.

The manual captures popular templates, resources and sectors, or state-wide variations in terms of procedures or requirements for setting up a company, and provides links to useful websites and references.

The book follows a hub-and-spoke approach in providing basic start-up-related information, descriptions of current practices and references to literature for further reading. Therefore, in addition to an informational view, the manual also offers a navigational view for the early stages of any start-up. It does not have to be sequentially read, and the reader can easily enter and exit the document at almost any point to consult it for any specific purpose.

While it may appear that consultants and lawyers can provide all the information given here, this manual offers a bird's-eye view (and more) of what entrepreneurs must be aware of and look out for. After all, a start-up is an entrepreneur's baby, and the best paediatrician's advice can be worthless without the parents' vigil.

IDEATION

1. Clarity

It is important to capture the idea for one's company precisely. A well-defined idea, commensurate to the level of detail required to establish a company, may take the founders some time to develop and to hone.

Most frequently, ideas for new ventures arise when an entrepreneur observes a market gap, indicating a demand that is currently not being met. Some ideas may be vision-driven and ahead of their time, and may not have a market yet in their current form. Ideas that may have been tested in other markets or sectors can, with a bit of tweaking, be made more relevant or appealing to another specific market or sector.

In the Indian context, ideas are typically classified as either local-market focused or global-market focused. Ideas for the local market in India are mostly directed at solving a specific problem that is unique to the country, and therefore, such ideas leverage existing or new technologies and local insights to frame their solution.

On the other hand, it is a very different game if one needs to develop a product or a solution for global market uptake. This approach needs to take into consideration the global competition in terms of both technology and market understanding. This is the primary reason why many ideas from India aimed at the global marketplace tend to be horizontal plays in terms of technology or offer a very specific domain-oriented solution with significant business and tech insight. Therefore, it is very important to define the scope of the idea in terms of its addressable market and its width and depth of operation.

At the inception, the clarity of scope may not be evident upfront, and the idea will require a fair amount of desk analysis, experimentation and field research to fine-tune it and build a proof of concept for market validation.

The scope creep challenge is frequently highlighted because it is mandatory to strike a fine balance between the broad scope of scalability of the business and the narrow scope of offering a solution to a specific problem. A product-based start-up is usually aligned towards a fine-grain scope, with limited width for building an asset-based solution. Services-based start-ups, on the other hand, focus on a bouquet of services to solve a problem or a use case, and they strive to bring together not only their own solutions but also third-party ones. It is important to remember these points on the scope dimension and to strike a balance between capital efficiency and product or solution completeness.

Any start-up in its early stage faces the twin challenges of optimizing money and time. All product-based start-ups spend money upfront to build an asset, which they monetize later. Therefore, the engineering cost of the product needs to be kept in check and hence, the need for finer scope control. Risk capital management is the model required here. In comparison, a service-based start-up starts making money at a much earlier stage and is more about working capital management than risk capital management.

The operating model for any start-up at its early stages is a blend of these models, at least till it finds its bearings in the market. 'Watch your cash' is the ideal slogan at this stage.

Falling in love with an idea

2. The Model Is Key

Clearly, creativity lies not in the idea but in the model that brings traction—evidence of market demand, or momentum in the market—in a new region or business sector. Of course, the idea must hit at the very base of the problem that it is setting out to solve and must avoid the distractions of scope creep and cash burn, as described above.

3. Fine-tuning

A landscape analysis in terms of desk-top research and market feedback for the idea is important and helps to further refine it for a business case.

Every inspirational idea may not translate into viable business plan; it is equally true that every great business does not thrive on an inspirational idea alone. A good business idea is typically a combination of novelty, usefulness and potential to scale.

PROMOTER SPEAK

Ideation

Is It Need-Driven?

K. Ganesh, Chairman, Portea Medical

Ideation does not start with an idea, but, rather, with a deep pain-point or a big problem. More often than not, it's not a want but a strong need that results in spotting a potential opportunity. It is important not to be carried away and fall in love with one's ideas in the ideation phase. A reality check is important and takes a lot of hard work. In this context, it is important to do a limited pilot or an MVP (minimum viable product) that could help in getting feedback.

Before we launched Portea Medical, we worked with more than 100 elderly and chronic patients to understand where the problem lay. Then we came up with ideas for solving those problems; often, these were suggested by the patients themselves. As founders, our job was to see how best to validate them and come up with ways to implement them. So, co-opting your potential consumers in the ideation process can go a long way in saving time and money by avoiding mistakes.

Finally, ideation is not just a one-time activity. It is a continuous learning process, and one needs to keep expanding and getting into contiguous areas to improve the offerings on an ongoing basis. At Portea Medical we started with two services: physiotherapy and nursing for the patients; within two years, we launched nine different services for the same patients.

Pivoting Based on Constraints to Scale

Aishwarya Singh, Co-founder and CEO, JustRide

JustRide started as an aggregator in the Rent-A-Car business with a fleet of eight cars. We leased the vehicles to commuters on an hourly and daily basis. The cars listed on our platform were owned by licensed leasing companies. We piloted the idea in Mumbai and the response was remarkable. Each car served roughly ten rides per week. The weekends were always sold out. After a few encouraging months, we scaled to 200 cars in four cities.

By the end of the year, we realized that our idea had a major limitation. Business was brisk but there were very few leasing companies in India. The limited supply of cars had put a cap on our growth.

We pivoted to a marketplace last winter. The switch helped us double the number of cars operational on our platform over the next quarter. But rebuilding products from scratch to suit market needs is easier said than done. We opened our platform to private car owners, helping them rent their vehicles when not in use. We trudged through confusion and chaos for weeks. Work doubled and we had to make some difficult choices.

The marketplace was not our expertise but a successful pivot gave us the opportunity to scale rapidly.

TEAM FORMATION

1. The Core Team

It is critical to have functional completeness in the core team. Typically, the core team consists of the founders and a few other members. In many start-up firms, there are two or three founders; it is advisable to keep the number under five.

An ideal mix for a core team includes a product expert or domain expert, a business person and an operations person. There are many other functional areas that may need leaders, but it is of utmost importance to have a blend of domain expertise, business-scaling expertise and operational experience in the founding team. It is also important to have some freshness in the team. A team should not be limited to or be weighed down by experts with their hangovers from the past. Innovation in a start-up is often brought in by an outsider to the sector in question, someone who reimagines the sector with a fresh outlook.

The team mix, in terms of product, business and operations, is driven by the business the firm is involved in, but it is quite useful to bring in the business development person early in the process so that the business can be evolved for a better product-market fit.

Blending cultures: A matter of perspective

2. The Founders' Agreement

In the present times, it is typical for a start-up company to have a founder's agreement.

A start-up is a full-time job, which entails hard work and many trade-offs. Therefore, it is always advisable for the founder to have someone else for company in his or her journey of entrepreneurship. However, it has often been observed that the presence of equal founders can lead to problems and that their power equation becomes a key factor determining how decisions are made in the firm. This is one potentially problematic area that should be addressed and resolved early on in the journey.

It is very important for the founders to agree on and document well the relative holdings of equity or ownership in the firm. It is also a good practice to declare the Intellectual Property Rights (IPR), if any, brought into the firm by each promoter and the exit terms for the IP created in the firm.

3. The CEO

Regardless of the number of founders in the company, it is important to designate *one* person as CEO right from the start to ensure speed and clarity in key strategic decisions and to help in conflict resolution.

PROMOTER SPEAK

Team Formation

What Kind of a Team Mix Should a Start-up Aim for?

Srikanth Iyer, Co-founder and CEO, HomeLane

The functional mix will depend on the kind of team being built—sales/marketing/product/tech/design/ops. For sales and ops, I would go with managers who have a good nose for numbers and can see the larger picture with regard to targets and related costs. They must also be great managers as both sales and ops are high-attrition domains as it is.

On the ground, the sales team needs to have people with tunnelled/blinker vision in respect of targets, as they are mostly individual performers. For ops, I would look for working with peers as being an important criterion.

ENTITY CREATION

1. Entity Structure

As most start-ups are in business for profit, the options available for entity structure are the Private Limited Company (LTD) and the Limited Liability Partnership (LLP). Not-for-profit ventures are generally registered under the Societies Registration Act.

It is a common practice to create a Private Limited Company for a start-up, because this is the entity type preferred by all Venture Capital firms (VCs) and public funds when they come into the picture later. The private limited entity demands the most regulatory disclosure compared to the LLP and other limited liability forms of registered entities.

The process for conversion of an LLP into a private limited firm is cumbersome and takes significant time and effort. Most VCs and public funds demand the creation of a Private Limited Company before they invest in a business.

2. Where to Register

Where one needs to register one's firm is a significant decision to make. For global market-focused firms, the entity is usually registered overseas to ensure ease of raising non-rupee funds.

An issue of evaluation or valuation

3. Holding Company and Regional Entities

Based on the market focus of the firm, it is also essential to differentiate a holding company from its regional operating firms, which are set up for sales or delivery.

PROMOTER SPEAK

Entity Creation

Setting Up a Garment Manufacturing Business

Anjali Schiavina, CEO, Mandala Apparels

We are a social enterprise founded in 2002 that manufactures organic, fair trade apparels and accessories using sustainable fibres. Through our transparent supply chain, we create global communities of farmers, manufacturers and end-consumers who are committed to a sustainable future.

As an organic certified company, finding the raw-material supplier was a challenge, especially with regard to compliance. As per certification, you need to be attentive that no genetically modified organism (GMO) seeds and certain pesticides are used, and GOTS-certified dyes are used for dyeing as well as printing. The factory must have an ETP, lead-free accessories, FSC-certified paper and use biodegradable polybags.

There are other challenges as well when it comes to khadi clothes. Khadi that is made by hand has a few drawbacks for the export markets—such as longer lead-time, the quality not being consistent, the fact that it is more expensive as the output per hour is low and how minimum wages are applied due to compliance. Therefore, buyers and suppliers tend to work on semi-automated looms.

With regards to chemical dyes, in case a supplier wants to promote vegetable dyes, he or she faces the same issues as mentioned above. Additionally, other issues, such as order volumes being much smaller and limited to the summer season, make the procedure not sustainable for both buyer and supplier.

It is very important to secure the supply chain with the required levels of compliance for organic clothing early in the venture before any scaling can happen in the organic clothing business from India.

Setting Up a New Alloy Manufacturing Plant

Amarnath Krishnamurthy, CEO, SG Industries

We are engaged in the manufacture of precision and special alloy castings. Before starting the venture, we studied its potential for almost one-and-a-half years. I visited similar units around the country and understood their business models. I discovered a few gaps in the existing companies and built a business to fill in those gaps. (for example, as a start-up, I never invested in a full-time design/engineering team. We built an initial team of three engineers to handle this function.

Initially, we employed many people but without the right skills. We did not focus on the shop-floor operations as well. When customers pointed out these issues, we quickly moved to fix them. We removed or reassigned people work based on their skills. Letting go of some people caused more difficulty in day-to-day operations, but in the end it was worth it. We spent months fine-tuning every subprocess in the four major processes of our manufacturing of special alloys.

Always train your team in developing a customer-servicing mindset rather than a product-manufacturing one (for instance, clear and timely replies to customers' queries, communicating in time if there is a delay in delivery, and so on). All this helps build a strong reputation for integrity with customers over time, which helps the business grow.

Should We Create an Overseas Entity

Mrigank Tripathi, founder and CEO, Qustn Technologies

A start-up's decision to incorporate/change domicile is usually driven by four key factors:

1. What markets will it be addressing/expecting to address.
2. Ease with which capital can be raised in/for those markets (all other things being equal), at higher valuations.
3. Ease of collecting recurring revenues—this is one of the biggest reasons for Indian SaaS companies to either incorporate abroad/set up subsidiaries abroad.
4. Future consideration of taxes—the US doesn't give any tax benefits to start-ups, but Singapore and other locations will be beneficial to start-ups.

We are a SaaS-based digital training start-up, incorporated in the US in 2015 for the same reasons, and I believe it was a mistake to have done so. Incorporating in the US is expensive and tedious, and unless there is a full-time presence there that can manage this, it is not advisable for small start-ups. Given today's point of effective management laws (POEM), it is advisable for companies to stay in India, do a monthly billing for Indian clients, use a third-party service for international clients (to manage recurring billing), and once the business is established and doing well, to choose a suitable domicile (keeping in mind the POEM laws).

EARLY-STAGE COMPLIANCE

The regulatory environment for start-ups has improved tremendously over the last few years, following initiatives taken by both the Central and state governments to ease the compliance load of starting a business in India. However, to avoid a problem that may arise later, compliance is an important aspect to pay attention to when the business is in its very early stages.

Many firms defer this work to a later stage, as they may not find it relevant in the early stages, and opt for a shorter route to reduce the process load in terms of costs and effort. But bypassing compliance matters often leads to bigger roadblocks in raising funds at a later stage or when scaling up globally. This is because most investors and customers at that stage demand clean books from a compliance perspective.

1. Key Aspects to Consider

1. *Labour Laws*
For many start-ups, the relevant registration comes under the Shops and Establishments Act, which is a state subject, that is each state has its own Act. The compliance

list under labour laws covers legislations for gratuity, Provident Fund, state insurance, migrant workers and construction workers. For start-ups that are not in the manufacturing sector, many of these blue-collar laws are not applicable.

The recent changes in the policy for start-ups allow self-certification for firms for the first three years of their operation. Inspection is conducted only when a specific complaint is made. There are state-wise variations here, so it is always good to check the state policy for the latest legislation. There are some states that allow self-certification only if the start-up is fostered by incubators or accelerators on the approved list of incubators in that state.

2. *Environmental Laws*
These are mostly applicable to a manufacturing entity or a service entity whose activities impact water or air. Here, self-certification is allowed as per the new policy guidelines, but one must check the specific notifications applicable, based on the region and sector of one's operations.

3. *Intellectual Property Rights*
The policy guidelines enable start-ups to claim rebates in filing of patents. The rules with respect to rebate claims are different from state to state, but as a rule, the rebate is applicable at the filing stage and at the award stage. It is important to note that the default nation for filing the patent depends on the citizenship of the inventor; the Indian inventor needs an approval from the Indian Patent Office to file his or her patent in another country. When and where to file one's patents are very important decisions. These decisions are primarily driven by the business and

technology context of the firm and involve drafting fees and filing fees for each patent filed for. As these amounts can be significant for an early stage start-up, there is a rebate given by the government for patent submissions.

4. *Closure*

There is a bankruptcy bill pending in Parliament for consideration of a ninety-day closure for winding up a failed entity. The winding up time and the directors' liability are the two major irritants for most start-ups (who either pivot on the business model to the next stage or fail at the fund-raising stage). It is very common for a company to create different sales entities for invoicing in different regions and for different customer and country requirements. Closure of the holding entity results in closure of all the operating entities and any other asset-holding entity too. As this is a long-drawn-out process, it is important to keep the entity structures simple and well defined. The holding entity cannot be closed until all the obligations are met in terms of financial, regulatory, contractual and employee-related matters. Any pending item or dispute reflects on the directors' track record and will restrict them from directorship at a new entity. The delays in winding up time (that can stretch for up to three years) and the extension of the Directors' Liability Act are hindrances to the 'fail fast' model of start-ups of the Internet era.

5. *Taxation*

The new policy guidelines allow profit exemption for a start-up for three years from the time of its registration. Moreover, there are no capital gains or angel taxes for the first three years.

The issues related to service tax and cross-border investments are highly contextual, so it would be pointless to suggest a specific approach towards them here. The taxes come under the purview of the Central or state governments, based on whether the company has a manufacturing activity (attracting excise tax), a finished product to trade (attracting value-added tax [VAT]) or offers a service (not tradable and therefore attracting service tax). The tax interpretation is done on a case-by-case basis, should the company's offering be a mix of service and product or a service that drives a product sale.

6. *Funding*
There are incentives available for start-ups in the form of grants and loans from different government agencies. It must be kept in mind that the definition of a start-up varies from state to state, as also the exemptions and incentives offered by each state to specific sectors.

There are matching funds from the state governments for start-ups funded by Central government grants, and some of the marketing expenses are reimbursed. These matching state government funds are top-up funds that help start-ups to solve their immediate cash challenges. Almost every state in India is creating such funds for nurturing start-ups.

7. *Public Procurement*
The biggest challenge faced by start-ups targeting government contracts are the clauses regarding prior experience and turnover requirements in public procurement policies in India. The guidelines put in place by the government of India provide exemption under

these clauses for start-ups in the manufacturing sector. There are also state-level procurement policies that have removed their high entry barriers to encourage start-up vendors. As this is a state-level and sector-level topic, it is difficult to elaborate on it beyond remarking that one has to explore public procurement as another customer segment in India now.

2. Well-defined Scope

Most firms are either a product play or a services play. Whatever their area of operation, for market positioning, a key decision to make pertains to what will be done within the company and what will be leveraged from outside.

The need for a sharp focus on what is created internally is to ensure that the scope is well defined. The scope creep challenge—when a project's scope can snowball in an uncontrolled manner—is a major reason why firms run out of cash.

The validation of a firm's scope is dependent on the core bet of the firm. One of the most important elements to check is whether or not the validation received is validation of the core bet. A general agreement or acceptance of an idea is very different from an agreement on the specific value proposition in business terms.

3. Determining Feasibility

Most of the firms today use a lean model of development, where they create a Minimum Viable Product (MVP) and get very early feedback from the users or prospective customers to fine-tune the product or service.

It is important to create a Proof of Concept (PoC) for feasibility so that it is demonstrated with evidence that such a product or service can be realized. Proof of business validation shows whether or not the product or service has business value or customer value.

PROMOTER SPEAK

Early-stage Compliance

Common Pitfalls to Avoid in the Early Stages

Ganapathy Venugopal, CEO, Axilor Ventures

Axilor Ventures is an accelerator and a seed fund. Axilor's accelerator programme is designed to help start-ups answer three simple questions: Whether they are working on something people want (validation of need), in what form are users willing to use it (validation of product) and what is the willingness to pay and who will pay for it (validation of business). We believe that these questions can be answered by founders themselves, quickly and without spending much capital.

Having seen more than thirty start-ups graduating through the accelerator programme in the last two years, I do find some common mistakes committed by the promoters of today. Here are some major mistakes that can be avoided:

1. *Setting up as a proprietorship or LLP (conversion to a private limited company is a long-drawn purpose)*: Setting up the right way is one of the most underrated aspects of a start-up. It is also the silent reason for many funding conversations falling through. While the actual mistakes

---

that start-ups make differ, three learnings are common: most start-ups overlook the importance of setting up right, most mistakes are avoidable, and the older the start-up, the more difficult it is to correct the errors it made.

2. *Having relatives who are unrelated to the business as directors with significant stakes*: This makes it difficult to bring an industry/functional expert to add business value and becomes a point of contention in the later rounds of funding.

3. *Not having founder agreements which result in founder fallouts when the entity changes*: This is one of the biggest issues in recent times as the founders differ in the strategy for scaling the business or seeking funds and render the firm dysfunctional due to their quarrels.

4. *Bringing capital into the company from a non-director in violation of the Companies Act (resulting in steep fines)*: In most cases, this is an act of ignorance. This makes institutional funding a challenge, and money cannot flow in till these are regularized.

5. *Not having employment agreements for founders*: The rules of engagement between the firm and founders need to be formalized. It cannot be left to goodwill and faith alone.

INTELLECTUAL PROPERTY RIGHTS

1. Introduction

Increasingly, start-ups in India are focusing on innovation and trying to explore how they can capitalize on the intellectual capital they generate. Intellectual Property (IP) is a dominant component of the intellectual capital/asset of the start-up venture that owns it, providing it a competitive edge.

One of the most significant challenges that start-ups in India face today is the lack of knowledge on their part to convert their work, ideas and inventions into IP. To generate value from their innovation efforts and obtain measurable returns on them, it is imperative for start-ups to develop a good understanding of effective management of IP and intangible assets. This section provides an overview of IP and guidelines for the start-up to manage its IP, both in-house and when engaging a third party.

2. Patents

A patent is an exclusive statutory right granted to an inventor(s) or patentee for an invention, which can be a product, composition of matter or a process, for a limited period by the government, in exchange for full disclosure of the invention. The inventor or owner of the patent gets the right to exclude others from making, using, selling or importing the patented product or process. Patent protection ensures that the invention cannot be made, used, distributed or sold on a commercial scale without the patent owner's consent. The patent is a territorial right, granted country by country, with most countries granting protection for a limited period, usually twenty years.

Most countries follow the process of awarding patents for products, processes, etc., to those who file the patent application first at the patent office (*first-to-file*). Therefore, filing of the patent application should not be deferred. One option is to fill a provisional patent application disclosing the essence of the invention; this allows the patentee to register his or her right of priority for the invention. The applicant gets twelve months to file the full application. If the inventor makes any public disclosure related to the invention in any form before filing the patent application, the invention is disqualified for a patent.

Think wild but stay grounded!

2.1 Subject Matter for Patent Protection

In most countries, patents are granted for inventions that are new devices, products, machines, processes, substances, composition of matter, or improvement to an existing invention. A relatively small improvement or change over what is already known or used may also be patentable. Some of what cannot be patented are theories, ideas, discoveries or scientific principles.

In recent times, large and small companies have been investing resources for developing new ideas for doing business using software or information technology that leads to significant business productivity, creating what are called business method patents. Whether such methods should be allowed patents or not is a subject of international discussion.

USA is one of the countries where a large number of business method patents have been granted in the last two decades. On the other hand, the European patent office is very conservative in allowing these patents; its regulation says that any 'schemes, rules and methods for performing mental acts, playing games or doing business, and programs for computers' are not patentable. Business method patents are well known in Japan and come under patentable subject matter.

However, such patents are not issued solely for business methods. A business method should contain a technical aspect that is both tangible and real for a patent to be awarded. According to the Indian Patent Act, any 'mathematical method or business method or a computer program or algorithms are not patentable'. However, the Indian Patent Office allows a patent for a new method if it solves a technical problem and an apparatus/system/device is developed from it.

2.2   Criteria for Patent Protection

For an invention to be eligible for patent protection, it should meet three main criteria, namely, usefulness to industry and society, novelty and presence of 'inventive step'.

Industrial Applicability (Utility or Usefulness)

For an invention to be patentable, it must be applicable for practical purposes; it cannot be purely theoretical. The invention should be able to contribute to the creation of the product/part of a product for which it was intended. And if the invention is intended to be a process or part of a process, it should be possible to carry that process out or to 'use' (the general term) it in practice. The 'industrial applicability' of an invention means that it can be used by technical means on a certain scale.

Novelty

Novelty is a fundamental requirement and an undisputed condition for patentability. An invention is new if it is not anticipated by the 'prior art', i.e., in general, all the knowledge that existed prior to the relevant filing or priority date of a patent application, whether it existed by way of written or oral disclosure.

Inventive Step (Non-Obviousness)

The question as to whether the invention 'would have been obvious to a person having ordinary skill in the art' is perhaps the most difficult of the standards to determine in examining a patent application for substance.

The inclusion of a requirement like this in patent legislation is based on the premise that protection should not be given to what is already known as part of the 'prior art' or something that a person with ordinary skill in the art could deduce as an obvious consequence.

3. Copyright

This describes the rights given to creators for their literary and artistic works, computer programs, databases, advertisements, maps, technical drawings, etc. Copyright law, however, protects only the form of expression of ideas and not the ideas themselves. The creativity protected by copyright law is the creativity in the choice and arrangement of such things as words, musical notes, colours and shapes. The creators of the original works are protected by copyright, and their heirs have certain basic rights. They have the exclusive right to use or authorize others to use the copyrighted work on agreed terms.

3.1 Subject Matter of Copyright Protection

Copyright protection includes every production in the literary, scientific and artistic domain, whatever the mode or form of expression. However, the work should be an original creation. This means that while the ideas in the work do not need to be new, the form in which they are expressed must be an original creation of the author. Copyright protection is independent of the perceived quality or value of the work. The work will be protected regardless of whether it is considered tasteful, whether it is judged to be a good or bad literary or musical work, and whether it serves the purpose for which it was intended, since the use to which a work may be put has nothing to do with its protection.

Exceptions to the general rule are made in copyright laws by specific enumeration; thus, laws and official decisions or the news of the day are generally excluded from copyright protection.

4. Trademarks

Trademarks are distinctive signs used to differentiate between identical or similar goods and services offered by different producers or service providers. A trademark offers protection to the owner of the mark by ensuring his exclusive right to use it to identify his goods or services, or to authorize another to use it against payment. In a larger sense, trademarks promote initiative and enterprise worldwide by rewarding their owners with recognition and financial profit.

Trademarks may consist of one or more words, letters or numerals, or a combination of all three. They may consist of drawings, symbols, three-dimensional shapes such as the outward form and packaging of goods, audible signs that may be musical or oral, distinguishing features or smells. Virtually any sign that can serve to distinguish one set of goods from another can constitute a trademark.

4.1 Criteria of Protection

Broadly, there are two different kinds of requirements that a sign must fulfil to serve as a trademark and they are reasonably standard throughout the world. The first kind relates to the basic function of a trademark, namely, its function to distinguish the products or services of one enterprise from those of others. The second kind pertains to the possible harmful effects of a trademark, should it be of a misleading character or in violation of public order or morality.

5. Industrial Designs

An industrial design is the ornamental or aesthetic aspect of an article, something that makes the article attractive and appealing, adding to its commercial value and marketability.

To be protected (under most national laws), an industrial design must appeal to the eye. This means that the protection is primarily for its aesthetic nature and does not extend to any technical features of the article made based on that design.

When an industrial design is protected, the owner—the person or entity that has registered the design—is assured of an exclusive right against unauthorized copying or imitation of the design by third parties. Industrial designs can be relatively simple and inexpensive to develop, and they are easily accessible to craftsmen as well as to small and medium-sized enterprises. In most countries, an industrial design must be registered to qualify for protection under industrial design law. The duration of protection varies from country to country and may be fifteen to twenty-five years.

6. Trade Secrets

Trade secrets consist of previously publicly unknown important and confidential data, information or compilations used in research or business; they include know-how, technologies, test methods, impurity profiles and other proprietary information that are not protected under any statutes. Trade secrets are useful to an enterprise and provide competitive advantage to their owner. The secrecy of the information must be maintained to conserve its trade secret status. Trade secret information may be disclosed or shared under the terms of a confidentiality agreement.

The table below provides a summary of the different types of intellectual property protection.

Table 1. A comparison of the four types of intellectual property protection

	Patent	Trademark	Trade Secret	Copyright
Information public	Yes	Yes	No	Sometimes
Duration	Up to 20 years from the filing date	Indefinite as long as the requirements for protection remain	Indefinite, for so long as kept secret and has independent value	For works created after Jan. 1, 1978; life of author plus 70 years; for corporate works, term is 95 years from publication or 120 years from creation, whichever is shorter
Subject matter eligible	Composition of matter, method of use, and process of production that is new, useful, and non-obvious	Words, names, numbers, symbols, devices, designs, sounds, and colors	Business and technical material, including ideas	Tangible expression of an idea, not the underlying idea itself; limits on non-artistic aspects
Owner's rights	Right to exclude others from making, using, selling, or offering for sale the invention	Right to exclude others from selling similar goods or services thereby trading off on the brand of the trademark holder	Right to exclude others from using or disclosing the trade secret	Exclusive rights to reproduce, prepare derivative works, distribute, public performance of, and display the work
Cost	Relatively expensive to obtain, police, and enforce	Inexpensive to obtain but can be expensive to police and enforce	Relatively inexpensive	Inexpensive to obtain but can be expensive to police and enforce

Source: http://www.nature.com/nbt/journal/v21/n2/fig_tab/nbt0203-201_T1.html

7. IP Management in Start-ups

7.1 Patent Portfolio Management

A start-up's patent portfolio is very critical for its business and strategy, holding immense potential for value creation by direct or indirect monetization. However, for successful value creation, the start-up's patent portfolio needs to be managed effectively. Understanding the size, content and focus areas of one's own portfolio for its effective management and appropriate exploitation is key.

7.2 IP Risk Management

A patent infringement lawsuit is extremely expensive and time consuming compared to other types of lawsuits. It is better to avoid patent infringement instead of defending a costly, burdensome lawsuit later. By identifying potential infringement issues upfront, one can prepare a risk mitigation plan to avoid infringing third-party-patented technology.

Even after due diligence to avoid infringement, the start-up must develop an elaborate process for the commercialization of newly developed product/processes and for dealing with infringement notices by a third party on any product or implemented manufacturing process.

The following are the objectives of the process:

- To identify the infringement risk of third-party patented technology
- To develop a risk mitigation plan for commercialization of newly developed products/processes in case of their overlap with third-party patented technology
- To decide between a defensive and offensive strategy in case of infringement

The following are the recommended key policies related to IP risk management:

- No staff of the start-up will knowingly use others' IP of any kind without written permission from the third parties, or without licensing the technology to avoid any possibility of infringement damages and contamination of start-up IP.
- A freedom-to-operate assessment must be conducted with the help of external IP experts for any new or modified product/process developed at the start-up before its use/commercialization to avoid any possibility of infringement damages.

7.3   Publication of Content Outside of Start-up Venture

Technical information and know-hows are generated on a continuous basis in an innovation-led start-up. The founders and staff of such organizations always strive to share their findings and results with the outside world to fetch recognition and applause for the start-up. Therefore, talks, presentations and papers at symposiums and conferences, and articles and reports on the company website and in leading journals by the start-up staff are very common. However, sharing information on intellectual assets may hinder their accrual of commercial exploitation value.

Conversion of intellectual assets into IP happens only by maintaining optimum confidentiality, and the assets should be protected so that the start-up can wield its monopoly on them at the appropriate opportunity. To strike an optimum balance between confidentiality and sharing of information on intellectual assets, a process of reviewing and obtaining IP clearance for all kinds of extramural publication must be put in practice at the start-up.

A formal clearance from the IP lead or group leader usually suffices; it may entail sanitization of documents to remove sensitive information from them.

7.4   Patent Search and Analytics

It is estimated that approximately 80 per cent of all the technical information that exists in the world lies in the form of patent publications. There are close to seventy million patent documents available and accessible in the global patent database. And, every month, over 200,000 patents (published and granted globally) are added to it. Currently, patents constitute the single most comprehensive collection of technological data for start-ups. They can help the start-up to:

- Identify and evaluate new and alternative technologies
- Keep ahead with the latest technologies in the field of business interest
- Find solutions to technical problems and ideas for innovation
- Locate business partners and identify niche markets
- Identify licensing and cross-licensing opportunities
- Evaluate IP of other companies for M&A, joint ventures and collaboration
- Identify talent from the list of inventors of patents of interest to the company
- Identify target companies for licensing and enforcement

Patent analytics, which means search and analysis of patent information, helps the start-up to make informed decisions when formulating strategies for developing new products/processes and can also guide its research efforts.

Thus, patent analytics can help a start-up to:

- Identify opportunities in technology and business
- Keep an eye on competitors for potential competition/partnership/M&A
- Avoid/mitigate risk of infringing
- Avoid reinventing the wheel
- Broaden the scope of invention under consideration
- Inspire new ideas, plan research activities
- Improve quality of invention disclosure

A patent portfolio analysis for a start-up is conducted to identify patent filing activity, the technology focus of its competitors, and the active players and preferred market for the product.

7.5   Confidentiality Management and Non-Disclosure

Trade secrets are information (technical or financial) related to the start-up that is not generally known to the public, as they are kept confidential within the start-up. They provide the company a competitive edge over its rivals. Unlike patents, trademarks, and copyrights, there is no specific legal protection provided to trade secrets in case of misappropriation if the company has not made reasonable attempts to keep them secret and confidential. In case of misappropriation of one's trade secret, it is important to demonstrate that sufficient efforts were made to protect and maintain the secrecy of the supposed trade secret. A failure to do so may render the allegation ineffective, irrespective of what means were employed by the defendant to acquire knowledge of the supposed trade secret or confidential information.

Employee Confidentiality Agreement

Start-ups should use several tools to protect trade secrets from being misappropriated, lost or stolen. The Employee Confidentiality Agreement is one such critical tool for attributing legal admissibility to the start-up's intended trade secrets.

The outcome of an employee confidentiality agreement management process should lead to:

- Retention of confidential information within the organization

- Restriction on the use of in-house-developed confidential information/know-how for any competitive advantage by third parties

The process of getting the employee's signature on the employee confidentiality agreement follows two phases:

1. At the time of joining, the employee signs the confidentiality agreement, which should be sent to the recruit along with the appointment letter. This agreement covers the confidential information non-disclosure clause. HR must ensure that all the existing employees sign the agreement to give this policy full retrospective effect.
2. At the time of an employee leaving the company, the separating employee is reminded about the confidentiality agreement, and HR obtains an undertaking from the employee (usually from middle and higher management) on a document specifying the sensitive, confidential and technology areas the employee has worked on.

The Confidentiality Classification System

For all internal and external documentation of information, technical or otherwise, a classified system of confidentiality is recommended.

A blanket confidentiality of a singular class or level imposed on all kinds of data and/or information can have adverse effects on the necessary flow of information and at the same time, can lead to inadvertent leakage of confidential information to an unintended audience. Therefore, there should be varying levels of confidentiality and security requirements, as this gives both the inventors and users of information not only a clear understanding of the level of risk from unwarranted exposure but also clear guidelines for dissemination of information to a concretely defined audience.

A start-up must develop a three-or four-level confidentiality classification system to manage public and confidential information, based on the sensitivity of the information:

- Public Information (Level 1):
  Accessible to all employees; can also be shared with third parties

- Confidential Information (Level 2):
  Accessible to all employees, but not to be distributed outside the company.

- Classified Information (Level 3):
  Accessible to the leadership team and owners of the documented information; remains out of bounds to the rest of the employees in the organization; owners can share the information with employees on a need-to-know basis.

An example of an undertaking of confidentiality and non-disclosure to be executed between the start-up and its personnel is provided on page 94.

8. Third-party Engagement

Maximizing value from the start-up's innovation performance for a given investment has always been an important concern for its founders and its senior management. Access to external know-how may improve the efficiency of internal activities and lead to enhanced revenues for the start-up. Studies have found a steady trend of start-ups with higher internal knowledge (measured by number of patents) being more actively involved in pursuing higher external linkages.

There are numerous possibilities and ways of engaging with external individuals and organizations (referred to as 'third parties'). Careful management of the different kinds of engagement processes and creation of the right matrix for determining the need for one type of engagement process over others, based on an understanding of these matrices, may thus provide sustainable competitive advantage to the start-up. As with real property, intellectual property can be bought, sold or licensed, and may be the subject of a variety of agreements.

Third Party Engagement Agreements: Typical Process

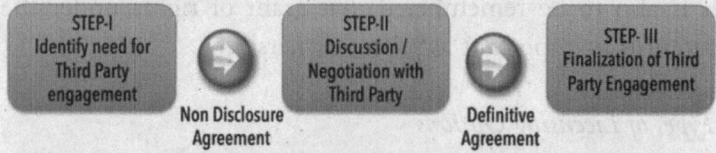

8.1   IPRs in Third-Party Engagements

General Overview
Best practices in IP management are built on a foundation of licensing and contracting expertise. A contract defines a bargain that the parties enter into, and, as such, defines the relationship and expectations of the parties. It is, therefore, critical to carefully draft contracts that clearly and objectively indicate the intentions of the parties, and to strive for direct, simple and accurate language rather than jargon.

Intellectual Property (IP)

The first step in drafting this section is to clearly define IP rights. This way, each party to the collaboration recognizes and acknowledges the other party's ownership of the contributed material.

The next step is to clearly establish how ownership of new intellectual property discovered under the project will be determined. Typically, three classes of new IP are possible:

- New IP solely discovered by party A
- New IP solely discovered by party B
- New IP jointly discovered by both parties

In collaborative work, many of the discoveries fall in the third class. A well-written collaborative agreement will address how and by whom the ownership determinations are to be made. It is also to be remembered that grant of rights under the patent is as important as patent ownership.

Types of Licensing Options

A licence can be a non-exclusive licence, a sole licence or an exclusive licence. A technology owner who grants a non-exclusive licence is permitted to grant the same or a similar licence to anyone else. However, the owner may not grant someone else a sole or exclusive licence.

Unlike a non-exclusive licence, an exclusive licence incorporates two promises. The first is the licence itself, i.e., a promise not to sue the researcher for patent infringement. The second is a promise by the technology owner to neither use the invention for herself/himself nor grant a licence to anyone else.

Co-exclusive licences cannot be granted outside of an identified group. A sole licence is similar to an exclusive licence, except that the technology owner retains the right to use the invention for herself/himself.

It is important to specify the licence grant's level of exclusivity in the agreement, the country or region to which it is exclusive and the time-period as well as the field for which it has been specified. Most organizations are reluctant to put their resources into an agreement if the organization is not assured of an exclusive licence, as their competitors may also seek the same licence.

Negotiating the grant of intellectual property is a key part of the collaborative agreement. A start-up must take time to think through it to negotiate for maximizing its IP ownership.

9. Details of IP Rights and Issues

9.1 Background IP and Foreground IP

These terms, sometimes found in agreements, are convenient labels to distinguish between different types of IP.

The term 'background IP' often comprises the following:

1. Background information consisting of confidential information, technical know-hows and other information known and owned by a party or over which a party has rights at the date of commencement of the agreement
2. Background intellectual property consisting of patents, copyrights and other similar rights, including applications, owned by a party or over which the party has rights at the date of commencement of the agreement

These defined terms are sometimes expanded to include information or IP generated after commencement of the agreement but which is not part of foreground information and foreground intellectual property because it is developed (for example) outside the scope of the agreement.

The term 'foreground IP' comprises the following:

1. Foreground information consisting of confidential information, technical know-hows and information generated by a party while working on or performing the defined research programme
2. Foreground intellectual property consisting of patents, copyrights and other similar rights, including applications, generated by a party while working on or performing the defined research programme

Applying these terms, the basic conclusion is as follows:

1. Background belongs to the party that introduces it
2. Foreground belongs to the party or parties involved in the research

Conclusion 1, mentioned above, is in essence no more than a statement that describes what is normally the default position and is usually included for the sake of avoiding doubt. The second item is of key importance, as it determines ownership of the IP generated by the research programme. Without such a clause, under IP laws, ownership of intellectual property would normally be with the creator instead of with the commissioner.

In some instances, ownership of foreground IP arising from a research programme remains with the creator, in which case the commissioner may need to obtain:

• A licence for the foreground IP, sometimes (particularly in the case of non-exclusive licences) on a royalty-free basis so that the commissioner can pursue its commercial activities making use of the research that he/she has funded

- An option to obtain such licence (particularly, but not always, an exclusive licence) on which financial and other terms are determined

Another common variation is that the creator of the foreground retains ownership but assigns the foreground if he/she decides not to file or prosecute a patent application; the creator retains or obtains a licence to use the foreground.

9.2 Intellectual Property Issues in R&D Agreements

These are dealt with in many ways, including the following:

Funding Party Owns and Controls IP

IP resulting from the R&D project may be owned by the funding party, with the research party retaining no interest or right to receive royalties from its use and having no say in how it is protected. This type of arrangement is most commonly found in consultancy agreements between a start-up and an academic scientist, for example, where the scientist is being paid to assist the start-up to solve a specific technical problem for the start-up. It is less common in contracts pertaining to funding a programme, where the research party will generally wish to retain some interests in the IP resulting from the project.

Funding Party Receives Licence to IP

The research party may own the IP resulting from the project, but the funding party receives an automatic licence to use and commercialize it. This licence might be non-exclusive but with an option for conversion into an exclusive licence, or exclusive in a specified field or territory. The funding party may be required to pay royalties or other payments to the research party for use or exploitation of the intellectual property.

In some cases, for example, in agreements between two biotech companies, it may be agreed that both parties will have commercialization rights, with territories or fields of applications being divided between them.

Funding Party Receives Option on Licence

Often, the preferred solution for a research party is to retain ownership of the intellectual property generated by the project and grant an option to the funding party to acquire a licence on commercial terms. Depending on the subject matter of the project, the licence may be exclusive or non-exclusive.

10. Typical IP Task Flow in a Tech Start-up

- Patent landscape analysis for the areas in which the start-up operates. Use of third party as they have professional-grade tools
- Identification of the core IP protection areas internally, which is based on the positioning and area of innovation where entry barriers need to be built
- Shortlisting of a few unique methods or processes that extend the state of the art discovered in the landscape analysis
- A specific patent search, through exploration of the relevant patent classes in detail to find the gaps in terms of scope and approach

- Development of a patent draft (if the inventor or the firm is interested in patenting, which is a bigger debate on strategy and not within the scope of this manual) including the synopsis, system description and probable claims in the patent
- Engagement of a patent drafting firm or a law firm with a patent filing service to develop a full-fledged patent claim and determine the countries to select for filing of the patent based on the business focus of the start-up. Most start-ups will pick USA for global business and India for local business.

(It is an expensive affair to file for patents in every country of one's operations, and it calls for examination of slightly different prior art results when drafting or defending such claims. It costs roughly 5000 USD per patent for one-time filing and search fees).

11. Summary

IP constitutes an important, strategic, competitive and financial asset for start-ups; therefore, start-ups must liberally invest in creating, protecting and monetizing it. In-house and external professional training programmes can be conducted for employees to further their understanding, interpretation and analysis of the value of IP, the techno-legal and business information contained in IP documents, and drafting of IP documents.

It is advisable to avail the services of high-class national and foreign experts and attorneys to seek guidance and advise and to secure IP rights for the start-up.

PROMOTER SPEAK

Intellectual Property Rights

Do We File Enough Patents in India?

Komal Preet, co-founder and patent drafter, Placitum IP

Placitum IP works with almost five new start-ups every year in addition to working with global law firms and large companies. These start-ups are mostly from the IT and software domains. Except for one start-up we worked with in the domain of optical system technology, it is very rare for hardware-and manufacturing-related start-ups from India to file for patents.

As a quick feedback, most start-ups believe that patenting is a very complicated and expensive procedure. Also, they start thinking about patenting only when they are planning to expand operations to the US or Europe, or when they are talking to investors in these geographies. A lack of awareness about patenting leads to such low rates of filing in India. Also, start-ups hesitate in investing their funds in patenting unless it is absolutely necessary.

It is important to think about protecting one's IPR early in the journey, and perhaps it is better done in the first two years of the start-up journey before business scaling happens.

Should You File Patents Overseas?

Vijaya Kumar Ivaturi (IVK), co-founder and CTO,
Crayon Data Pte

One of the hottest debates in a start-up is about where to file the patents after deciding to file for it in the first place.

For an Indian citizen, the decided location would be India for the first-time filing of any patent; one has to take a clearance from the Indian patent office if the first filing is to be done overseas. For Crayon Data, we are required to file in Singapore first as it is a Singapore-registered company and is part-funded by the Singapore government agency. In our case, the inventors are Indian citizens while the intentions are to be filed in Singapore first. This is a typical situation in many cross-border start-ups, and you need to account for this clearance-process time in India before filing abroad.

We have now moved to a regime where it is 'first to file'— not 'first to invent'. I suggest a landscape analysis of patents in the relevant subclasses in the first eighteen months of a start-up journey, in order to ensure that the firm has an overall view of what is state of the art, and whether their invention is pushing the boundary. It is, of course, a matter of a start-up's business and tech strategy whether they want to publish or patent their novel methods.

As you would typically pitch to early-stage customers much before you would even think of filing a patent, it is important to ensure that all the innovation-related aspects of the product are *not* disclosed on public forums. The companies' website, videos and white papers should not, in general, disclose all the methods to the public as it invalidates any claims for patenting later. All publicly available information becomes prior art for the patent.

It is important to choose the countries in which you want to file patents based on business reasons—it is typical to file patents in those countries where you expect significant business to come from. This is a long and tedious process, and a costly one as well. Many firms merely file for patents to get the advantage of a 'filed' status before they raise funds. Many patent offices know this trick, and their default response is to reject all the claims made in the patent and see whether you will ever come back to them with a response! The office actions from patent offices of different countries may list different prior-art citations and, therefore, the work on the start-up side is more if more countries are to be covered.

THE GENERAL DATA PROTECTION REGULATION, 'GDPR': AN OVERVIEW

AIM: GDPR Law, a consumer-centric piece of legislation, replaces the Data Protection Directive 95/46/EC and aims to standardize protection for the consumer and the personal data of EU member states and EU citizens. It lays down rules related to the protection of natural persons with regards to the processing of personal data and also the free movement of personal data.

The emergence of GDPR as the main reference standard for compliance is due to the fact that it came into effect on 25 May 2018; it is latest standard built after four years of detailed study of comparable standards across the world, and its regulatory framework has been crafted with consumer rights and privacy as the centre of focus.

While there is no data privacy law in India yet, India's draft paper on data privacy is heavily modelled on the GDPR regime in the EU, and therefore it may be necessary to put some basic controls in place, broadly based on the GDPR, until such time as India's own law comes into place. And indeed, such controls are frequently insisted upon by Indian customers.

GDPR consists of 11 chapters and 91 articles.

Two key roles have been classified and defined as follows under the regulation:

1. Controller: Any legal or natural person who (alone or jointly with others) determines the purpose and method of processing personal data.
2. Processor: Any legal or natural person who processes data on behalf of the Controller.

In the context of customer contracts, the Controller is the primary party and person who contracts with the customer is the service provider. The Processor is the person who processes the data of customers on behalf of the Controller. GDPR lays down the direct obligations of the data 'Controller' and 'Processor'. Processors will be subject to civil claims and penalties, as GDPR introduces obligations for the Data Processor for the first time. As an example, if company A uses company B for its payroll processing, the role of Data Controller is mapped to company A as the owner of the data, while the role of Data Processor is mapped to company B as a service provider.

Static analysis of GDPR – key parameters:

Privacy policy

Privacy notice is required to be provided at the time of collection of data, when the data is obtained directly from the Data Subject. The Data Subject is a natural person whose data/information is collected.

Data Protection Officers (DPO)

DPO appointment is mandatory only for those Processors and Controllers whose core activities consist of processing operations which require regular and systematic monitoring of Data Subjects on a large scale, or of special categories of data or data relating to criminal convictions and offences. DPOs ensure that all important aspects are met, by monitoring internal compliance, informing and advising on data protection obligations, providing advice regarding Data Protection Impact Assessments (DPIAs) and acting as a contact point for Data Subjects and the supervisory authority. A DPO can be an existing employee or an externally appointed person and must report to highest level of the management.

Record keeping

It is duty of the Controller or the Controller's authorized representative (as the case may be) to maintain records of all activities. Article 30 of the GDPR says an organization must keep written (electronic counts as written here) records of the following items and be ready to provide these records to the authorities on request:

- contact details of all Controllers, Processors and DPOs
- the methods and processes by which information is gathered
- the categories of information collected, and
- the categories of Subject, purpose of collection, etc.

Policy debates in GDPR:

Territorial scope and applicability

GDPR makes its applicability very clear. One of the major changes it has brought about is in the regulatory landscape in the matter of data privacy. GDPR now applies to any business in the world that sells goods or services to EU countries, regardless of the company's location or size. It applies to any organization in the world that for any reason observes and records the behaviour or collects personal data of residents of EU countries. GDPR applies globally, and companies outside EU will have to comply with the regulation if they process personal data of EU Data Subjects in connection with their offers of goods or services to them or if they monitor their behaviour in the EU.

Coverage

GDPR is vast in scope and applies to organizations outside the EU that offer goods or services to individuals in the EU. However, it does not apply to certain activities, including data processing covered by law enforcement directives of individual countries, data processing for national security purposes and data processing carried out by individuals purely for personal/household activities. Both personal data and sensitive personal data are covered by GDPR.

Data of Persons vs Right to Access

Data of identifiable natural person: an identifiable person is one who can be identified, directly or indirectly, in particular by reference to an identification number or by reference to one or more factors specific to his physical, physiological, mental, economic, cultural or social identity. As per the expanded policy of GDPR, Data Subjects reserve the right to know what kind of data is processed by the Controller. Data erasure is another right that vests with Data Subjects; it now grants them the authority to erase their data any time. This is to enable transparency among Data Subjects, and this right has been provided in order to empower them with respect to how their data is collected, stored, used and erased.

Applicability to residents

Recital 14 of the GDPR reads as follows:

'The processing of personal data is designed to serve man; the principles and rules on the protection of individuals with regard to the processing of their personal data should, whatever the nationality or residence of natural persons, respect their fundamental rights and freedoms, notably their right to the protection of personal data.'

The protection afforded by this regulation should apply to natural persons, whatever their nationality or place of residence, in relation to the processing of their personal data. GDPR does not cover the processing of personal data that concerns legal persons, and in particular undertakings established as legal persons, including the name, the form, and the contact details of the legal person.

Retrospective application

GDPR is not retroactive; however, it will apply to historical breaches discovered after its implementation. The European

Union adopted a two-year transition period in order to provide businesses with the time needed to ensure they are up to speed with GDPR. Companies were expected to map their data across their organizations in order to implement the policy in its true spirit.

Exemptions

GDPR does not apply when data is processed during the course of an activity that falls outside of the law of the European Union.

GDPR does not apply to individuals who process data for personal or household activity.

GDPR does not apply to government agencies and law enforcement agencies when data is collected and processed for prevention, investigation, detection or prosecution of criminal offences, for execution of criminal penalties or for preventing threats to public safety.

GDPR does not apply to the processing of personal data by member states of the EU for activities under the scope of Chapter 2, Title V, of the Treaty on European Union, which deals with the common foreign and security policies for member states of the EU.

Cross-border flow of data

Personal data is permitted to be transferred to a third country or international organization, subject to compliance with set conditions, including conditions for onward transfer by the data exporter and data importer. GDPR allows for data transfers to countries whose legal regime is deemed by the European Commission as providing for an 'adequate' level of personal data protection through a 'valid transfer mechanism'. In the absence of an adequacy decision, however, transfers are also allowed outside non-EU states under certain circumstances, such as by use of standard contractual clauses or binding corporate rules (BCRs).

Data localization

There are no data localization requirements under the GDPR since it offers flexible tools for different business models and transfer situations.

Sector-specific application

GDPR is directly applicable in each member state and will lead to a greater degree of data protection harmonization across EU nations.

Across sectors, in the consent system, firms must clearly outline the purposes for which they collect data and seek additional consent if they want to share the information with third parties. In short, the aim of GDPR is to ensure that customers retain the rights over their own data. Vendors cannot disassociate themselves from obligations towards data access. The regulation imposes end-to-end accountability to ensure that client data stays well protected, as the enforcement is not only for an entity but for all its support functions too to embrace compliance.

Consent under GDPR

Data Subjects should give clear and explicit consent for their personal data to be processed for a specific purpose. The consent shall no longer be illegible and filled with legalese difficult for Data Subjects to understand. Consent must always be specific and informed.

The Data Subject reserves the right to refuse consent without detriment, and must be able to withdraw consent, request to delete or to be forgotten easily at any time. It also means consent should be unbundled from other terms and conditions wherever possible. The clause related to 'right to be forgotten' is an important one, as the Data Controller is responsible for deletion of specific users' historical data and the associated linkages from the systems of record.

The GDPR does not set a specific time limit for consent. Consent is likely to degrade over time, but how long it lasts will depend on the context. The GDPR does not prevent a third party acting on behalf of individuals to indicate their consent.

Consent from children

Article 8 states that if services are requested and delivered over the internet and you want to rely on consent rather than on another lawful basis for your processing, you must get parental consent for children under thirteen (which is the age set by the UK in its Data Protection Act 2018). Under GDPR, the default age at which a person is no longer considered a child is sixteen; however, member states reserve the right to adjust the limit to anywhere between thirteen and sixteen. Data Controllers, therefore, must know the age of consent, in particular of individual member states, and cannot seek consent from anyone under that specified age. If you choose to rely on children's consent, you will need to implement age-verification measures and make 'reasonable efforts' to verify parental responsibility for those under the relevant age. However, consent of a parental figure is not needed if the data is collected for counselling for preventive services which may be offered to the child directly.

Notice

The GDPR mandates a Data Protection Impact Assessment when introducing new technologies or in the case of large-scale or systematic profiling or processing of data in today's data-driven world. In the context of apps, once an app is installed, the information related to disclosure, consent, usage and storage of user data should never be more than 'two taps away'. The regulation examines in detail the various exceptions to providing notice under GDPR, including in instances where data is obtained indirectly and where providing notice proves impossible or involves disproportionate effort. Article 13 and 14 state that content notices, preferably, should include different means to communicate with the Controller; notices should specify the 'relevant' legal bases; and the categories of recipients should be as specific as possible. Where free services are being provided, 'information must be provided prior to, rather than after, sign-up,' given that Article 13(1) requires provision of the information 'at the time when the personal data are obtained.' A notification of changes should always be communicated by way of an appropriate modality specifically devoted to those changes.

Legitimate grounds for processing

Recital 39 of the GDPR touches upon the lawfulness, fairness, transparency and purpose of personal data processing: any personal data processing must be lawful and fair, and it should be transparent to Data Subjects as to what personal data regarding them are being processed. Additionally, the principle of transparency requires that any information and communication regarding personal data processing is easily accessible and easy to understand. The need to use clear and plain language has been explicitly mentioned in the scope of the purposes of data processing.

Storage/data quality

Article 5 of the GDPR mandates steps to be taken to ensure that personal data that is inaccurate, having regard to the purposes for which it is processed, is erased or rectified without delay, which means that storage of such data is not warranted. The Controller must be able to document having followed reasonable best practices for data quality, and Article 5 notes that the Controller shall be responsible for and be able to demonstrate compliance. Organizations should not keep personal data for longer than needed. Storing personal data beyond the time requirements of the initially stated purpose is allowed only if it is for public-interest archiving, scientific or historical research, or statistical purposes.

Participation rights

The right to data portability allows individuals to obtain and reuse their personal data for their own purposes across different services. This right only applies to information the individual has provided to a Controller. Under the right to erasure, individuals can make a request for erasure verbally or in writing. This right is not absolute and only applies in certain circumstances.

Accountability

GDPR requires that the Controller is responsible for ensuring adherence to privacy principles. Moreover, it requires that the organization must demonstrate compliance with all the principles. It explicitly mentions that data shall be kept 'no longer than necessary' for the purpose for which it is being collected. The GDPR explicitly says that where proportionate, implementing data protection policies is one of the measures you can take to ensure, and demonstrate, compliance. Privacy by design has long been seen as a good-practice approach when designing new products, processes and systems that use personal data. Under the heading 'Data Protection by Design and by Default,' the GDPR legally requires you to take this approach.

Data protection by design and default is an integral element of being accountable. It is about embedding data protection into everything you do, throughout all your processing operations. The GDPR suggests measures that may be appropriate, such as minimizing the data you collect, applying pseudonymization techniques, and improving security features.

Remedies

Chapter 8 of the GDPR covers various rights, remedies and penalties which may be levied in the event of any breach of the law.

Under Article 82 of the GDPR, any person who has suffered material or non-material damage as a result of an infringement of the regulation has the right to receive compensation from the Controller or Processor for the damage suffered.

Data Subjects have the right to lodge complaints concerning the processing of their personal data with a DPA in the member state in which they live or work, or in the member state in which the alleged infringement occurred. The DPA is required to keep the Data Subject informed on the progress and outcome of the complaint.

Proceedings against a Controller or Processor shall be brought before the courts of the member state where the Controller or Processor has an establishment. Alternatively, such proceedings may be brought before the courts of the member state where the Data Subject has his or her habitual residence, unless the Controller or Processor is a public authority of a member state acting in the exercise of its public powers.

Key note to readers: This paper aims to analyse how the advent of EU GDPR has brought the digital world to a new era, giving it a new meaning and understanding in a channelized way. GDPR has been hailed as the most dynamic game-changing regulation in the era of digitalization, leaving no stone unturned to protect the rights of Data Subjects and provide limitless remedies related thereto . . .

Start-ups and GDPR compliance in India:

For many start-ups, the applicability of GDPR is based on what kind of data they deal with in their business. While it is difficult to define specific actions for GDPR compliance in a generic fashion, there are some key points to consider and find answers to before implementing any changes.

1. The start-up must define the role it plays in the GDPR context—is the start-up a Data Controller or a Data

Processor, or both? There are many start-ups which are data driven in their solutions, and most of the time they may fall under the Data Processor rather than the Data Controller role, which is often played by the customer. There are many b2c start-ups who may be the data controllers for user data, and it is important to map the data pipeline in the business to identify these roles and stages.

2. The main demand from Indian customers concerns data residency, and this is about where the data actually resides in terms of its geographical location. For many Indian customers, the popular request is that their data should be in India even if the delivery is cloud based. This removes for them the headache of classifying different data sets and ascertaining which sets constitute personal information and which sets public information. They insist that all the data be in India so that the task of data jurisdiction is simplified for them.

3. In the post-GDPR era, almost everyone with a web front for their business displays the usage of data they collect and the purpose thereof. This is to make sure that they inform the users about what they collect, why they collect it and what they do with user data. However, the level of disclosure and the means to withdraw consent may not be fully defined, but it is almost a standard practice to comply with the consent and limitation of purpose clauses in the GDPR.

4. In certain sectors, it is often insisted in the business contracts that the role and position of the person responsible for data be defined. It is a good practice to define and publish this role in the start-up context. The role of a data officer is important in any matter related to data privacy and security, and this is one position that

may need a formal publication of the role; currently, many start-ups have flexible, flat and fluidic organizational structures and roles.

5. One of the most complex and debated clauses in the GDPR is the data retiring model. When a user withdraws his or her consent for data usage, the Data Controller needs to ensure that those data sets and associated links are removed and has to certify their removal to the authorities. While it may be easier to identify, isolate and delete specific user data, it is not going to be a trivial effort to remove the derived data sets and learning from the specific user data. As the data is often federated, cleansed, curated and transformed for real-world usage by software algorithms, it is going to be a daunting task to comply with this clause. It is in general agreed that reasonable and full action taken to this effect will convince the data regulatory authority concerned as to compliance, but an audit trail needs to be maintained. For the moment, it is important to keep the original or raw user data independent of the transformed data to implement this retiring model. What is to be done is also heavily dependent on the specific region or jurisdiction applicable, in terms of the country in question, and therefore one cannot be very prescriptive here.

As a first step, many data-driven or AI/ML start-ups begin with a customer contract audit by a data privacy expert to find out the gaps in their processes and the risks associated with them. As these matters are closely related to data security too, it may be better if the data security and data management teams get involved in these efforts and map the above five key areas to their specific context to formulate their compliance plan.

MARKETING

1. Introduction

For any start-up, marketing is a crucial element among those that drive business growth. Driving and prioritizing marketing deliverables is necessary for meeting business targets and creating a long-term brand that consumers love.

Practically, marketing a start-up to everyone is a waste of time and money. The key is to identify a niche target market and go after market share aggressively. Is the business B2B, B2C or B2B2C? Which are the target geographies? Who are the key stakeholders? What defines them? In a B2B scenario, what are the target verticals?

Traditionally, marketing has been understood in terms of the AIDAS funnel, i.e., Awareness, Interest, Desire, Action and Satisfaction. However, with the increasing complexity of the market and its omnichannel characteristic, this funnel has become more *circular* than *linear*. Today, any customer who is not happy with a product or service rants about it on social media, and this could negatively affect awareness and interest for a start-up. Equally, a happy customer can as quickly bring in referral customers simply through a tweet.

2. Defining the Target Market

There are four main factors to consider when deciding on a target market:

1. *Market size*: Is the target market a regional demographic? Is it a specific gender? Does it consist of children? The goal is to determine the number of potential customers in one's target market.
2. *Market wealth*: Does this market have the money to spend on the start-up's product?
3. *Market competition*: Is the market saturated, meaning, are their many competitors?
4. *Value proposition*: Is the value proposition unique enough to cut through the noise?

With a well-defined market, a keyword list, to be used primarily for blogging, social media and the company website, can be built. Essentially, the list of words or phrases must be highly relevant to the brand being built. A pertinent question to ask at this stage is, 'What would someone type into Google to find the start-up website?'

There are free tools available to find the keywords already sending traffic to the start-up website. The core keywords can then be run through Google's Keyword Tool and Uber Suggest. Keywords with low competition and high traffic are the best, because while many people are searching for those keywords, they display few results.

3. Defining Success for the Start-up

Success is different for every start-up. For instance, for start-up A, success could be 500 new signups per month, while for start-up B, it could be revenues of Rs 5 crore per month. Whatever the start-up's idea of success, it must be defined early and rigidly. It must be written down and sent to the entire team. Everyone the founders are working with must know the definition of success for the start-up so that they can prepare to work towards it.

Consistency is important. It does not matter if success is defined by signups, revenues, profits or anything else one can think of. One definition must be picked and adhered to, and commitment to this must be unwavering.

4. Setting a Budget

How much can the start-up afford to spend on its marketing strategy?

More than the total budget, it is the division of the budget that should be carefully planned. Perhaps, the start-up's blog has been its most powerful tool to date, and the intention is to invest 40 per cent of the budget on it. Or perhaps, 35 per cent of the budget is to be spent on developing a new eBook or online course.

5. Defining the Audience

The definition can be narrowed down by asking what kind of an audience is most crucial to the start-up's success. In most cases, the audience can be broadly categorized as prospects, talent, media and investors. The start-up marketing strategy should be capable of identifying the category of audience most crucial at the current stage of the business and how best to communicate with them.

6. Key Elements of Marketing

In a practical context, marketing today can be perceived as a sum of three key elements: demand generation, brand building and customer engagement. They are not mutually exclusive, but the distinct categorization helps a company to focus its efforts and go about building its marketing teams.

Depending on its sector of operation and on whether it is B2B or B2C, the start-up might need to concentrate on different activities at different times. A B2B business might first want to build overall brand awareness for the company and then generate leads for individual products. A consumer-focused start-up, on the other hand, might want to start with a Google search campaign and then invest in brand building with offline efforts. A travel-focused start-up might initially focus all its efforts on customer engagement and retention to ensure repeat business. Investment in marketing should never be postponed. It takes investment as well as time and effort before one can see results.

6.1   Demand Generation

Business targets in terms of revenues or customers need to be broken down into demand that is needed on a weekly or monthly basis. Marketing teams need to plan online and offline campaigns to drive interest and generate this demand.

Online marketing broadly encompasses the following features:

- *Search Engine Marketing (SEM)*: Users with a ready need that the start-up might be able to address can be targeted using SEM. It should be ensured that the entire audience identified for the start-up is targeted through search engines such as Google, Bing and Yahoo. It must be checked whether consumers are reaching out to the start-up from their desktops, mobiles or offline call centres. Bidding and targeting the right keywords for the start-up's product or service and showing users the right message to ensure they are converted into customers is the essence of SEM.

- *Facebook, LinkedIn and other paid social media*: Paid ads on social media are increasingly turning out to be a major source of online leads for all businesses. A B2B brand might want to reach out to decision makers through a LinkedIn ad or an InMail reach-out campaign, while a B2C brand can invest in a sponsored news feed that piques the interest of the target audience. Social media also provides options to filter out interests, location, age and other factors so that brands can segment and target their specific audience.

- *Search Engine Optimization (SEO)*: This refers to a set of marketing efforts to improve visibility for a product or service in organic or unpaid searches. The leads from here tend to give the best conversions and hence the best 'cost of customer acquisition' too. Content marketing, video transcripts, articles, blogs, the URL structure for the start-up's website and a host of other factors go into building this. The key is to get consumers interested in what the start-up offers and wait for them to get back to the start-up on their own.

- *Display campaigns*: Banners and other advertising units across Google, Yahoo and other publishers can get ads to new audiences. These campaigns can be part of the lead-generation activities as well as part of the brand campaigns that go along with other offline media for brand building.

- *Mobile app installs and other new initiatives*: Looking at the digital landscape and what it is today, it is crucial to keep an eye out for the newest trends. Ads on Instagram might be the best tool for one brand, while driving app installs might be the sole objective for another.

Offline marketing includes what has traditionally been referred to as Above The Line (ATL) and Below The Line (BTL) marketing efforts. While these approaches are mainly used for brand building, they could also complement the demand-generation efforts for a product/location or service. These efforts could include:

- TV, print, radio and outdoor
- PR and Online Reputation Management (ORM) through portals and review sites
- BTL actions through events, conferences and on-ground brand activation ideas

Following are some tips for a basic digital marketing model for the initial stages of a business:

For B2C

- Targeted search and Facebook campaigns
- Creating social media presence on key platforms for awareness and engagement
- Ensuring that website and landing pages are optimized for web and mobile experiences

- Putting in place basic brand guidelines to ensure that logo, colours and branding are consistent
- Paying close attention to customer feedback to fine-tune product, pricing and positioning

For B2B

- Identifying events, conferences, partners and platforms to reach out to influencers and decision makers
- Creating inbound marketing leads through webinars, blogs or thought-leadership portals
- Leading nurturing efforts through email automation to convert warm leads into hot leads
- Creating high-impact pitch decks, videos and other collaterals that elucidate the value proposition
- Leveraging existing clients for feedback and referrals through roadshows or testimonials

6.2 Brand Building

This encompasses a 360-degree range of marketing ideas that communicate how the brand addresses a consumer need. Whether it is an enterprise solution that helps the organization serve its employees better or a taxi service that helps the customer get to office, it is important to get the offer positioning and messaging right and strive to deliver this consistently. Brand advertising does not typically yield results in the short term. A good practice is to start investing in brand-building efforts in targeted, low-cost ways and scale it up to include ATL media as access to funds increases. Some metrics that could be used as indicators of brand campaign performance are as follows:

- Direct traffic to website, which indicates the number of unique users who typed in the brand URL to reach the website, absolute numbers and mix of overall traffic
- Brand search volumes, which indicate the number of unique users who searched for the brand name on search engines
- Positive sentiment on social media in research reports and PR

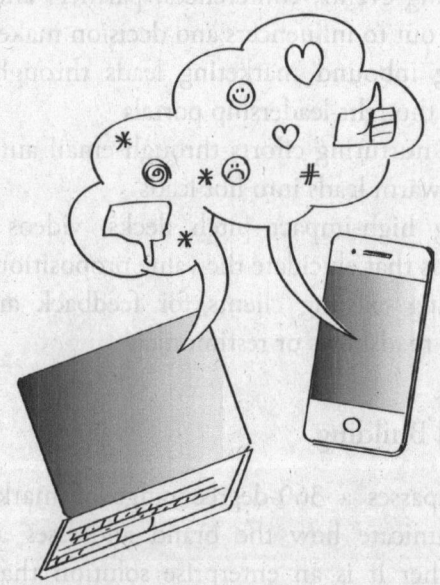

Telling compelling stories in the post-truth era

6.3 Customer Engagement

A laser-sharp focus on customer delight and engagement is key to a successful business. Marketing needs to drive, audit and ensure that all the processes—right from the message that plays on the call-centre number to how the service is delivered to the consumer—are streamlined to deliver a consistent and delightful experience to the consumers every single time. *What's in it for me?* is a question every consumer will ask the brand. Reaching out to the existing customer base for feedback, ideas and inputs will keep customers engaged and have them coming back for more.

Approaches to building excellent marketing teams can vary, from hiring a passionate marketer as part of the core team right at the beginning to working with agencies and vendors until a later phase. Hiring specialists for demand generation might be important in the first few months, whereas hiring a senior generalist who can take a more holistic approach to marketing would be important as the business grows.

Useful links:

- https://www.hubspot.com/inbound-marketing
- http://www.kaushik.net/avinash/search-engine-optimization-metrics-analytics-questions-answers/
- http://www.marketmotive.com/
- http://sethgodin.typepad.com/

7. Go-To Market Strategy

Most early-stage firms get classified as B2B players or B2C players. It is important to differentiate between selling to an enterprise and selling to an end consumer.

When the buyer is an enterprise, the selling cycle is often longer as one needs to traverse the organizational structure, discovering who—and in which roles—will influence or buy the product. At an enterprise, there are many checks and balances related to current vendors, differentiated value for adding a new vendor, integration with their existing systems and adherence to the procurement process.

In a B2C scenario, it is a very different dynamic, as one is looking for a channel through which to engage the end consumer, one which is capable of discovering, engaging and monetizing the segment of users who fit the use case of the product. It is also about appealing to the buying behaviour of consumers rather than just offering them a rich or differently featured version of the product. The classical stages of awareness, consideration, trial and buying by the consumer need to be mapped to the marketing and sales strategy of the firm to decide on the scaling model. The SaaS model is very popular now in this segment.

In a B2B scenario, it is crucial to pay attention to the differences across diverse industrial sectors in the buying process. It is also preferable to make business development investments sector by sector to map the process and develop a strategy that engages customers. This is the reason why many early-stage firms focus on a few sectors in which they have had prior experience before they try out new sectors.

Here, indirect demand generation efforts through business partners and channel agents can help the company make an entry in a new sector. This is one business development investment—one that goes beyond the core team's capabilities—that needs to happen. In fact, in the initial years, such a partner can be a member of the core team to help the company address the challenges of a new sector and build initial traction. And at scale stage, someone may even be appointed to take on the role of overseeing channel marketing or alliance management.

In both B2B and B2C scenarios, it is important for the core team to get involved intimately in the early-stage deals. This creates a feedback loop for product-market fit and enables the firm to fine-tune the back-end processes to meet the market requirements in terms of both content and priority.

In the case of B2B, it must be kept in mind that large clients tend to have competitive RFP processes, so it is critical to make sure that the firm is qualified to receive the RFP. There could be significant requirements of company size, antecedents, financial stability, etc., to participate in such processes. It then makes sense to co-create a solution with a large client. However, it is important to make sure that the firm is not stuck with any 'exclusivity' clause that may prevent it from growing.

For B2B, international markets may turn out to be a very expensive affair if the product requires direct pitching. It is much more cost-effective to get a sales/channel partner who can work on a predominantly commission-based model.

PROMOTER SPEAK

Marketing

Building Organic Growth

Nikesh Garera, co-founder and CEO, EventsHigh

EventsHigh is a marketplace where consumers can discover all events and activities in one place, organized via location, interest and social circle. Organizers use our CRM to sell tickets, promote their event to the right audience and manage their end-to-end workflow for digital presence.

Our approach was to hack the supplier inventory via tech and build the consumer side, as opposed to the conventional approach of building the supplier side of the marketplace, giving us a strong edge over our competitors in respect of inventory coverage and users. This helped us in getting 10x better coverage compared to our competitors.

We built a scalable approach to crawling event inventory from the Web, de-duping, categorizing it to 10,000+ interests and localities and indexing it in Google. Because of our hyperlocal and interest-specific comprehensiveness, Google started ranking us higher in the search results for every event- and activity-related query, resulting now in more than a million monthly unique visits to eventshigh.com. With significant consumer traction behind us, we now understand the events that people are interested in, and we use this data to intelligently on-board and integrate suppliers (organizers) for ticketing and promotion revenue.

Cracking organic growth requires patience and exploring lots of channels. It took us one-and-a-half years to reach from 0 to 200,000 monthly unique visits, and six months to go from 200,000 to 1.2 million unique visits. It takes time for network effects to form, and it is well worth the wait and efforts for building a defensible business and sustaining the growth in the long run.

PRODUCT MANAGEMENT FOR INDIAN START-UPS—A PRIMER

Purpose of project management

Product management is a cross-functional role and strives to build a holistic view of the product for the firm. It typically represents the customer's voice inside the company and drives the roadmap from a market viewpoint by keeping the balance between the external opportunities and the firm's vision and capabilities, and also laying them on both budget and timeline axes.

The Indian context

Product management maps the market needs and builds an outline of product expectations. It does take some iterations, both internally and externally, before it becomes a requirements doc or user stories and backlog repository. The challenge in product management lies in framing the problem rather than in solving it with a toolset. It does take a change in mindset, effort and patience to develop a problem-domain view for the firm.

In India, the typical tendency is to ask customers for their requirements and build a specific solution for the same. The dominant mindset of a services economy is about fulfilment of customer requirements, and there are many opportunities in a developing economy for such services. Product management as a discipline never developed as a core competency in India, as many solutions here are reactive, custom built and service-centric in nature. With the rise of local market demand, and regarding its breadth and depth in both domain and tech usage, the need for product management is emerging as a critical factor for the new-age entrepreneur.

Definition and scope

Globally, the scope of product management is about answering the WHY and WHAT of the product from a market perspective. The issues related to HOW and WHEN should follow these purpose and relevance queries. The study and analysis of the answers obtained would cover the aspects of the need for the product, its purpose, utility or impact.

This exercise demands a fully dedicated role most of the time, for which reason there are some role definitions for this work in the industry. There are some well-established norms in the global business context for these role definitions, and there are some subtle differences too with respect to the titles given to the personnel who perform these roles.

Product manager: This role defines and drives the vision of the product and its roadmap. This is a typically a market facing business role.

Product owner: This role leans more towards the engineering function—to craft, plan and manage product development and features delivery in an engineering context.

Product marketing: This role is for developing the positioning, messaging and collaterals for product promotion and sales support.

In the Indian context, the importance of problem identification and validation of the problem statement from the market perspective is finding acceptance and priority among entrepreneurs. This is because we are slowly moving towards local products development and scaling these products for the global markets. While it is much easier to understand the need for a product in a local context, it becomes a little more challenging when it comes to global markets, as establishing the global demand for a product cannot be based on local Indian market appreciation. This is one of the reasons why product management roles are getting attention and being staffed with people with global or MNC exposure.

The firm's positioning in the product offering-versus-service offering problem plays an essential role in deciding the role and positioning of the product management role in the firm.

In this context, the current landscape in India contains three different types of firms:

1. *Pure product play firms*

   These firms appreciate the need for a product management role as the product in its genesis should address a valid, relevant and pressing customer problem

We explain the distinction using the case study methodology from a real product firm, Comviva Technologies, headquartered in Gurgoan, Haryana, with a large presence in Bengaluru, Karnataka.

The who's who in the case study are:

Manoranjan Mohapatra (Mao) – CEO of Comviva Technologies

Girish Pai – Product Manager in the Messaging Business Solutions unit of Comviva Technologies

Joe Manuel – Product Manager in the Messaging Business Solutions unit of Comviva Technologies

Ramana Kumar – Head of Engineering in the Messaging Business Solutions unit of Comviva Technologies

Ganesh Jayadevan – SVP, Messaging Solutions, Comviva Tech

A brief success: the importance of market study

'It's like happy hour at a pub,' says Girish Pai, product manager at Comviva Technologies. 'If you visit a pub on a Monday, Tuesday or Wednesday, especially between 4 p.m. and 6 p.m., it will likely be happy hour there. They may even serve roasted peanuts on the house. But if you go to the same pub on a Friday or Saturday, you will notice you don't get the same offer.'

Girish was describing the weekly cyclicality of the demand for beer. The same applies to voice calls too, he says. Interestingly, voice calling has a pattern that is not only based on the day of the week but also on the 24-hour day.

The worldwide pattern in voice calling shows two peaks and two troughs on most days. Weekday behaviour and weekend behaviour would be different, as would the holiday calling pattern too.

Telephony load is measured in Erlangs. An Erlang plot for a particular day will show two peaks: one between 7 a.m. and 11 a.m., and the other between 6 p.m. and 9 p.m. This leaves two troughs: one between 11 a.m. and 6 p.m., and the other post 9 p.m. till about 7 a.m. the next day.

The implication of these varying loads has an impact on radio design. Radio equipment must be sized for peak capacity, even though utilization is not flat. Operators incur capital expenditure (on towers, base-station controller (BSC), cabling, etc.) and operational costs in the form of expenditure on electricity, diesel, maintenance, etc.

Dynamic pricing is a standard technique (like happy hour) to smoothen peaks and reduce the depth of the trough. The only question on Girish's mind was how this could be done efficiently in the case of telecom networks.

Ericsson had an in-call solution, which was heavy on hardware had to provide very high reliability and availability, also known as five 9s or 99.999% in a telco solution, that would connect to the mobile switching centre or MSC. The integration was also an elaborate effort—again, because of the nature of the solution. The solution had to be inserted into the network as a thing-in-the-middle (TITM), and that was expensive and time consuming. Ericsson's price point was a couple of million USD per license.

With call rates being low in India and Africa, operators were not willing to buy an expensive solution. Return-on-investment (ROI) considerations did not justify the investment.

But Girish sensed there was an opportunity if the capex and integration issues could be taken care of. Girish and Ramana Kumar (head of engineering) approached Prasad, the CTO of an Indian telco major. Prasad came up with a suggestion for an offline solution that addressed many of the pain points in the Ericsson solution. The solution was a low-capex, low-cost one regarding network integration.

Girish was excited about taking it to market. He had sold the idea inside the company, and the sales forces were continually checking with him for sales collaterals. Both Girish and the sales teams had targets to meet. He wrote up a sales collateral and sent it to his Head of Department, Ganesh Jayadevan, for review. Ganesh asked for a point-by-point comparison with the Ericsson solution. He listed the following aspects to be compared: technology, integration, operational, service interfaces and end-customer user experience.

The point-by-point comparisons in terms of functionality were on par, except that the user interface comparison revealed something: the Ericsson solution had a voice announcement letting users know of the current discount just upon dialling. An offline solution would not allow that as voice circuits were not in the path. The solution, while being technically feasible, was suboptimal in the user experience aspect. Users could not blindly call hoping they would get a meaningful discount at the time of calling.

To Ganesh, this had to be solved. His point was simple. Operators are moving away from capex to opex, and therefore one of the revenue models would have to be revenue share or a per-subscriber fee, which would put the burden of success of the product both on the operator as well as on the supplier of technology. While the sale was a b2b one, the b2c angle, with consideration for the user, had to be addressed. Ganesh's argument was a simple value-chain one: unless the end user experiences value, the points that followed would not experience value. And therefore, for the dynamic discounting product to be successful for Comviva, success had to begin at the point of service delivery to the end user.

This tension internal to the organization was finally solved, with Girish and Ramana finding an offline method to convey the offered discount to the customer by a mechanism called CBC (cell broadcast centre) that would send out a message to all users attached to a particular cell.

It took the team the next one month to re-engineer the product to add CBC, but the story ended well. In the two subsequent years, Comviva flooded the African market with the dynamic discounting product, replacing Huawei and winning bids against Ericsson.

In hindsight:

If we compare this case study with the revenue-plus one (covered later on Page 78), it is clear that this effort was based on a much more robust understanding of certain fundamentals. Consumer behaviour was nailed down, and it was a good fit for the market need. The benefits to the consumer and to the telco operator were well articulated.

Also, the team got lucky with the fact that an OEM major such as Ericsson had a similarly functioning product, which further validated the need for such a product. But the Ericsson product was expensive and had a bunch of inefficiencies, which was the opportunity for this team.

Where they did not do well was in the following: dynamic discounting had an excellent run for two years, but subsequently could not sell any more licenses. With the fall in calling rates, voice calling had become a commodity, and discounting made no sense. This is a risk that the team did not understand at that time. It pointed to a lack of rigorous market and trends study on their part.

2. *Product-led services firms*

o   They balance a general or perceived need in the
market regarding a product with specific customer
contexts by taking customer inputs before building
solutions. Therefore, the completion loop is customer
specific. The product management function is used
to find, scope and select the generic product or basic
product specification, but the product is rarely sold
in its original version.

The tech man can operate in an island

Ganesh Jayadevan, who used to work at Wipro handling
large accounts, lapped up an opportunity in a company called
Comviva Technologies to work on innovation. With over
fifteen years of work experience and a few patents under his
belt, his hands were itching to create something new and make
an impact. Comviva was a software products vendor in the
telecom space and was mostly into messaging and payments.
While the existing lines of business were doing well and even
growing, the CEO of Comviva, Mao, knew they would face
headwinds in the next few years. Ganesh's aspirations and
Comviva's needs fitted very well. Another added advantage
was that Comviva had an excellent relationship with significant
telco operations in India, Africa and the Middle East.

Soon after joining Comviva, Ganesh got right into the
act. He got connected with all the major customers and did
a tour of India and Africa. He hit it off with Prasad, the
VP of Technology with a major telco operator. Ganesh was
overawed by Prasad's detailed knowledge of telco networks.
And reciprocally, Prasad often complimented Ganesh for

---

his experience in building products. Prasad asked Ganesh to build a product to enhance average revenue per user (ARPU) by making special offers to customers. He offered to share technical documents for the various interfaces. Ganesh was itching to get something done, and Prasad was keen on making an impact on the ARPU side for his telco.

Ganesh and his team created a product called Revenue Plus. Ganesh found a senior manager, Ramana Kumar, who put together a team consisting of a DB expert, backend Java and frontend GUI skills, and built the product iteratively. Prasad shared plenty of requirements with Ganesh, and Ganesh played the role of a product manager, writing specifications and making a roadmap. Everyone was busy and happy. They even ran trials in Karnataka and Kerala with the help of the telco's technical team. They ran many campaigns among small populations, and the results were positive.

The next step was commercialization. Prasad referred the matter to the marketing office (CMO). Ideally, given Comviva's close relationship with the telco, the issue should have been an open-and-shut case. But slowly, Ganesh started to realize there was more to it than just building a fully functioning product that delivered results.

The telco had outsourced all of its IT to another major IT provider. Ganesh came to know of the implications of this relationship only after one year of joining Comviva. The IT provider had the first right of refusal for any IT requirement. IBM was providing marketing support, but it was apparently not as good as Prasad would have liked it to be. When the matter was discussed with procurement, Prasad (note that he was part of the CTO organization) was taken in context. Comviva product did more than IBM's, but not enough to justify replacing of existing tools, overcoming IBM's objections and incurring the cost of replacement that included retraining of staff. The costs and risks were seen to be higher than the proposed benefits.

But Ganesh was not about to give up. He had built visibility for the solution inside the organization, and even the CEO had nice things to say about it. He was not about to give up his baby.

Having built the product, the next logical step would be to sell the product to other operators and other geographies. Ganesh crisscrossed India, Africa and south-east Asia. He met with all the major operators in these regions. Some were enthusiastic as they did not have a system to enhance ARPU as part of their marketing. Others who had tools welcomed the idea that the product did more than what they were using. Some others wondered if they had the skills to put in place such a practice.

Ganesh used to feel good after every meeting with the operators. But gradually, after two years, his gung-ho enthusiasm began to get leavened by a sense of reality, and he wondered if he was ever going to get a purchase order.

The thought of shelving the product was too much to bear for Ganesh and his team.

In hindsight:

This is a very typical story of the journey of an engineer who has spent too many years in core technology and has little exposure to the world of technology business. It is a trial by fire, which a few survive—the lucky ones do, but many don't.

The product owner and his team were highly enthusiastic and committed, and wanted to make a mark. Ganesh and his team were ambitious and loved the freedom they had at the workplace. But while passion is great and self-belief necessary, they are not sufficient to build a product that will succeed.

Not once during their product journey was the phrase 'market requirement' mentioned. Not once did they do a risk analysis that may have accompanied an ROI assessment.

Many decisions had been taken based on Ganesh and his team's personal rapport with a user, and based on assurances without verification. The other persona, the buyer, is absent almost until the very end of the engagement with the major telco. This is a common pitfall, even among start-ups where a product or a service is built delivering value to the user but has no clear path to revenues, which essentially means that validation of the revenue model has not been given enough importance. There are success stories, such as of some social media platforms, where a buyer shows up later in the game. But we would like to caution that these are remote exceptions rather than the rule. The path to revenues from multiple customers is an essential piece of the puzzle and has to be addressed throughout the process. 'If you build it, they will come,' is likely to prove an anti-pattern.

Another pitfall this story reveals is that the team took positive signals from probably polite conversations. The product owner makes a twenty-hour trip from Bengaluru to Nairobi and is treated well by the host. Perhaps, after a few knocks, a recalibration of how to read customer response will be learned, but leaving such learning to time is expensive.

Organization mapping is a beneficial exercise. Understanding who is who—the key decision makers (KDMs), influencers, those-for and those-against—must be done. What becomes clear after a while is that all the focus has gone into building the product and not enough into the sales process. Good sales folks are great at figuring out how to navigate the customer world, and their antennae are usually up and receptive to the politics of a customer. A strong sales persona at Comviva would have figured out the IBM angle.

Unfortunately, organizations dominated by engineering don't allow sales to influence product strategy or tactics.

One underlying theme that emerges in this case study is the lack of an old hand in product management who could have guided Ganesh and his team. In some ways, one could say that this was the state of the industry—it was mostly a service industry comprising IT players and even captives in India who mainly did the last legs of the development process and were not exposed to the initial stages of product conceptualization and building. We call the exercise product management these days.

3. *Pure services firms*

    o   They are used to a model of implementation based on specific customer requirements. Their mindset is less to focus on the problem domain on their own than to focus on being skills-driven in a solution mode. As they mature in their offerings, they will move into a more formal exercise of product management definition and roadmaps.

Role and activity dimensions

The focus of the product manager is to stay in the problem domain and develop arguments for the WHAT and WHY. Unless the situation demands getting into the HOW of the problem to discuss the architectural choices and tool selection to resolve the price, margin and release-time tradeoffs, the product manager's role is restricted to being one of the internal buyers representing the customer interest. Once the product is released in the market, there may be interactions related to customer feedback and market traction aspects. Therefore, the product manager is more involved in the planning side of the business than in the execution side.

Functional interfaces

The product manager plays the role of an orchestrator to blend in the different functional views to make a business plan for the product. Customer or market input is primary here. The other aspects include product marketing, engineering, and customer support or field teams for providing insights into how the product is behaving in the market and to balance this out with what the product is designed to do. The feedback from early adopters of the product is crucial to make these tradeoffs and pivot if needed.

Organizational identity

In smaller firms, the product manager role reports to the CEO. In larger firms, it reports to the CPO or LOB head. It is ideal to have this function report to a business role and not to an engineering role.

The long-term journey calls for rigour

The mobile phone ushered in a revolution in the developing world like no other. What was the privilege of a few was now accessible to almost the entire population. Within this revolution, the smartphone was yet another—a computer in the hand of every man, which could do much more than just make calls. This everyone understands.

The mobile phone was also becoming a tool for direct marketing using SMS to customers, amongst the various other ATL (above-the-line) and BTL (below-the-line) strategies. The effectiveness of SMS promotions had always been questionable, though. This type of promotion suffered from two challenges: users were bombarded with messages, leading to crowding out; secondly, what attention a message got from the user was always in doubt.

Smartphone prices had been dropping, and the price points had come within reach of the population that could only afford the feature phone until then. The CMO of a significant telco in India, in an invited talk, pointed out an exciting behavioural change among mobile users. 'From the ear to the eye,' was his major observation, describing how users were looking at the display much more than before.

For Joe and Girish, who were product managers in the messaging business, this gave them an idea. Girish, who had helped build Revenue Plus, was continually looking for plans to put the product to use and to monetize. He hypothesized that if at the end of a call, a notification is sent to the user about her balance, wouldn't the attention on the balance be an opportunity to send a promotion?

Joe socialized the idea with major and trusted customers. Feedback was good. But, unlike the dynamic discounting product, this product was something none of the potential customers wanted to license. By 2013-14, revenue-share trends and sharing of cost-savings had become innovative models prevalent in the telecom industry. Telecom operators were fast becoming marketing organizations that owned the brand and the customer base, while vendors with solutions would get access to customers. Fair or foul, the big telcos wanted to de-risk themselves and pass the risk onto the vendors. It was up to the vendors to make their products successful, and they would get a share of the spoils whenever there was an upside.

For the messaging business unit, this was a challenge. They were used to selling licences and did not have to bother about whether the customer monetized them or not.

Not only did the product managers now have to think in the context of b2c and user interactions with the product, but they also had to do something they were not used to doing earlier: measure product effectiveness, do the necessary accounting and therefore the revenue dashboards, and perform the reconciliation process with the customer, which would enable them to book revenues.

There was no one in the team who had expertise in running a revenue-share business. All the thinking and subsequent operationalizing of the offering had to be done from scratch. In adopting a new business model there would be plenty of mistakes made, which could impact the customer's business and subsequently the revenues to Girish's unit.

Ganesh wrote down his choices: a) he could try and do it alone with his inexperienced team, b) hire someone who had experience in revenue-share models, or c) partner with another business unit that had expertise in running a revenue-share business, but he would have to share up to 50 per cent of his revenue with the partner.

What should Ganesh do?

He discussed the dilemma with his boss. The boss's advice was to go with c). This was an excellent opportunity for a company-wide effort to leverage the existing strengths of the company, even though revenue would have to be saved. After deliberating with the team, they realized that this was the wise choice to make.

Comviva sold iEOCN (Interactive End of Call Notification) to three customers, and it became a cash cow for years to come. But iEOCN also suffered the same fate as dynamic discounting. With falling calling rates, operators started to offer unlimited calling, and the need for subscribers to look at their mobile to watch their balance just vanished.

In Hindsight:

From the idea-to-product point of view, this was a textbook case that had the elements of design thinking, consumer behaviour, market analysis, dealing with shifting business models, and internal tensions and politics that are a reality in all companies. A start-up may not see the internal considerations at the start, but surely, as the number of products grow and organizations build around specialization, these factors would doubtless be revealed.

One way around the revenue considerations would have been to have two separate accounting methods: internal business reporting, which would allow for double counting, and another P&L number, which would be consolidated across the company to remove duplicate reporting. This would have allowed the department good at operations as well as the product unit to report the entire revenue as theirs (win-win), but on the other hand, it could lead to severe inefficiencies. Ganesh had approached Mao (who was also the CEO) to permit this to happen, but his request was turned down. It would have also disturbed the organizational strategy of having each business unit run as a P&L.

This case points to a serious gap in strategy. Nowhere is the lifetime of the product considered. There are two reasons for this undesirable omission in the thought process. All the focus was on making revenues for the year, which many companies get consumed with. Business units are rewarded on meeting yearly targets, and it would be difficult to get them to give much thought to the long-term future. A company-wide strategy function that is not incentivized on y-o-y targets would need to take this up. This is an organizational problem.

Artifacts produced in the course of product management

The role owns and creates the following artifacts as part of the product management function.

Pre-development phase artifacts:

- Vision and goals of the product {PreD}—problem statement beyond convenience
- Themes of the product roadmap {PreD}
- User stories (in the old world, it would be PRD) {PreD}
- Roadmap and metrics definition {PreD}
- Negotiation with sister teams to get priority on their roadmaps {PreD}
- Working with UX to ensure designs are ready for the sprint {PreD}

In-development phase artifacts:

- Backlog Management {D}
- Prioritization during sprint {D}

Post-development phase artifacts:

- Positioning {PoDev}
- Pricing {PoDev}
- Beta Process definition {PoDev}
- Sales readiness {PoDev}
- Launch {PoDev}
- Unit economics
- Metrics tracking {PoDev}

KPIs used, and the growth path

Typical KPIs for product management are:

Topline -Revenues
Engagement -Users
Bottom-line -Contribution margin
LTV (Long-term customer value)
CSAT
Market share and Competition analysis
Backlog
Pipeline

The growth path for the product management function is as follows:

PM--- → Senior PM--- → Director, Product--- → Senior Dir, Product-- → VP, Product-- → SVP, Products- → CPO

The external ecosystem interfaces

The goal of product management is to understand the stated and unstated customer needs that are unmet. Therefore, product management needs to interface with customers, marketing and partners carefully, to understand what creates pull for the product.

Decision boundaries and budget

Product management needs to own the P&L for the product under its scope. However, the organizational structure of the company determines the decision trees, reporting mechanism and budget allocation source. In India, all this typically comes under the marketing or business development function.

India-specific challenges in product management

Getting drafted into solution building for the customer

The ability of the product manager to stand up to organizational pressure to develop the problem domain and not just implement what the customer is saying is crucial in the Indian context. Therefore, this function needs senior management support and independence from the functions of engineering.

The ability to understand and articulate what the customer needs rather than what customer wants is the hallmark of a mature product management function.

Sales support efforts post sales for the customer

It is essential to obtain the raw feedback from customers to understand the gap between what the market needs and what is envisioned for the product. However, it is important to stay away from the mindset of creating the requirements on the go for every customer or from supporting specific customer situations on account of delivery challenges.

Lack of maturity in mapping the global market needs

There is a shortage of talent in product management for b2b businesses in India. Every market is unique, and therefore, while one needs global experience in product management in the developed markets, one also needs to have a fine-grain understanding of the local market system. There is also a tendency not to use global practices or products brought in by a third party but to build a local and custom solution with the available resources.

Interference from founders

Trust is very important for this function to succeed. Founders' block is a real risk here. The product manager must be able to assert his or her way in the organization and not become a casualty in the power structure of the firm. For most start-ups, the first product manager is usually one of the founders, and it forces the alignment of vision and traction in the market. The mix of the founding team is critical here.

Shallow market data

Loose, lazy and limited product definition is an impediment to successful product management. There is also an on-the-job learning model here, as this function is not just a hard skill that can be taught and scaled. It needs mentorship and field presence to make it succeed in the Indian context.

Q&A with Amit Jain,
Managing Director, Shingora Textiles Ltd and
Co-founder and CEO of Zenscale Ludhiana, India

1. **How do you classify your firm? As pure product play, product-led services or pure services?**
    Zenscale is a pure product play firm.

2. **Is there a product management function in your firm? (You may have a different name for it, but this is the role that represents the market view).**
    Yes, there is.

3. **Whom does this role report to? (CMO, CEO or Business head)**
    The CEO.

4. **What are the typical result areas for this role? (How is it measured for success?)**
    The number of customer complaints in a given period of time has a direct bearing on the product quality.

5. **Are there any specific instances you can quote for India-specific products? (A popular comment is that India pays for its needs and not for wants – current pain focus.)**
    Our product addresses the need of this 'exact' India – needs vs wants; high value & low cost. Zenscale is an ERP/ Business management solution especially targeted at SME manufacturing businesses. Modular, cloud-based, pay-per-use model.

6. **If there is any advice you have got for an Indian entrepreneur?**
    Dream Big; Work Hard; Believe in yourself! The difference between a dive and jump is that the dive is head first (all in)! Always dive and never jump!

Key Recommendations

1. Creation of a product management team close to the market being served.
2. Co-location of the product management team with the product engineering team for cross learning, empathy and deeper interactions, which are often iterative.
3. Development of a product feature prioritization model based on b2b, or with a b2b segment focus driven by end-user engagement, virality, market parity, compliance, extensibility, delight and usability.

FUNDING

1. Seed Funding

In general, seed funds are given by people known to the promoter group or by someone who believes in the product idea even before it has shown proof of market traction. In such cases, the investor—while he trusts the product idea—is betting mostly on the capability of the team. Often, the product idea morphs into something else in response to the market feedback that comes in. It is this ability of the start-up team to pivot a good idea around to create a good business that the seed investor bets on. At this point, the firm is either in a pre-revenue or early-revenue stage.

The common practice is to use a convertible note as the financing instrument if there is no clear proof point or model to help arrive at a valuation for the firm. This means the firm will consider the current investment amount as debt in its books, with the option of conversion into equity at the next stage of financing. As the seed investor is taking a much higher risk in investing in the firm at the current stage, it is a well-established practice to provide a 15–20 per cent discount to this investor at the next stage of valuation during conversion of the debt into equity.

There are many aspects to how and when this conversion takes place, and it is important to pay attention to the specific terms that trigger (or do not trigger) a qualified financing. The early-stage funding scenarios keep changing in markets across the world and have a bearing on the preference for convertible notes. Beyond the seed stage of funding, what is popular now is a mix of equity, venture debt and convertible notes.

A sample convertible note document is provided in the templates section.

A typical investment of Rs 10 lakh to Rs 30 lakh is done at this stage, and some of the seed investors may play an active role in the firm to get more customer traction and, in some cases, may request for a mentor to be taken on to provide advice. In most cases, mentors are compensated with an equity of 1–3 per cent, paid in tranches, for their help in growing the firm.

The next stage of financing typically happens around twelve months later, as it is expected that the firm will still not be operationally profitable. At this stage, the burn rate needed for growth is more than the run rate in billing.

2. Angel Funding

This is the first institutional finance stage for many early-stage ventures, and perhaps, their first major dilution in equity too. Proof of business value is needed at this stage. Also required are some early revenues or significant customer traction indicating the proof point of customer value and price discovery. The funding range is typically between Rs 70 lakh and Rs 7 crore ($100,000–$1 million) at this stage for dilution of 15–29 per cent of equity.

In this round, there is a common term sheet but many individual investors on the capital table. Board representation of at least one seat is usually demanded by the investor(s), and a formal legal diligence is also done for the customer contracts, entity formation and regulatory papers.

This stage is also the phase in which formal business status reporting starts, demanding a full-time finance person at the firm to handle governance and reporting at the firm.

The runway to the next stage of finance (series A) for growth capital is typically eighteen months, though at some firms it is just twelve months.

It is to be noted that every time funds are raised, some percentage dilution in equity occurs; this usually takes some bandwidth away from the promoters.

The funds are invested for growth as well as product tuning at this angel-funding stage. This means the firm may not be profitable yet and will need some more financing later.

3. Series A

This is a growth-stage round for scaling the business, when the investors expect to see a certain run rate in terms of revenues and an order pipeline for the next one or two quarters.

The minimum funding made by VCs is usually Rs 14 crore ($2 million) for a 20 per cent stake in the investee company. The start-up will therefore need to show revenues in excess of Rs 7 crore ($1 million) before getting to this stage. In a B2C scenario, significant customer or user traction is factored into this pricing round, and in a B2B scenario, the lead client or IP substitutes for the revenues-volume goal.

The typical lead time to close this round is about four months. Funding is typically for a maximum runway of twenty-four months.

At this stage, the operational efficiencies at scale as well as the demand-side pipeline creation are important. Unit economics and repeat business measures are the key metrics considered here.

At this point, the strategy for scaling matters as it must work out a balance between market share and profit share. In the case of B2C businesses, for example, even while it may still be a user growth-driven market with good adoption and repeat rates, profitability will be sacrificed for market growth. On the other hand, in B2B businesses, the deals at the customer project level may turn profitable, but the investments required in new sectors and regions will keep the firm in net loss.

It is relatively easier to raise money in India in the early stages of a start-up, but the USA is better for exits. In either case, it is important to raise funds from wherever they are available, as global fund flows change very often. Start-ups must keep the cash chest filled without being too fussy about where the funds come from.

PROMOTER SPEAK

Funding

Using Inorganic Route to Fund Raising

Ashish Nichani and Sudarsan Metla, founding team, Place of Origin, a Craftsvilla company

Founded by Ashish Nichani and Sudarsan Metla in early 2015, PlaceofOrigin.in is India's first and largest online marketplace for speciality ethnic foods. We have on-boarded 300+ iconic local food brands from twenty-three states of India on to our curated platform. With over 3500+ unique foods available online, PlaceofOrigin connects food lovers looking for local specialities with small-food manufacturers looking to sustain and grow their business beyond traditional markets.

By mid-2015, PlaceofOrigin was the first and only start-up to successfully graduate from the very first accelerator-programme batch of Axilor Ventures, a new start-up accelerator founded by Kris Gopalakrishnan, Shibulal and Prof. Tarun Khanna of Harvard.

Utilizing personal savings and a small seed investment from Axilor Ventures, we focused on building the foundation—on-boarding quality sellers and content, a customized e-commerce platform, solid processes, a viable digital marketing template and a customer experience roadmap.

Once we had the foundation in place, we started to reach out to the major angel investment groups as well as early-stage VC funds. Without any external support or mentor, we managed to reach out to over sixty key angels/VCs/groups. Our pitch focused on the uniqueness of our concept, our business metrics based on all our experiments as well a clear roadmap towards unit profitability—everything an investor should know about a business.

To our surprise, we found that most investors had a blinkered focus only on rapid scaling, with a scary disinterest in actually building a viable business model. And given the recent issues with hyperlocal food-delivery models, the food sector wasn't their preferred 'flavour of the season'. Some even wanted to superimpose their vision on our business!

The dominant philosophy was: Accept the funds, burn at a faster rate, show scale and then get back into the market to raise more funds within the next few months itself!

So while we needed the funds on offer, we didn't agree with the associated baggage of their investment philosophy. A chance meeting during this period changed our situation dramatically.

While contacting listed angel investors, we had reached out to Manoj and Monica Gupta from Craftsvilla. Over the course of our first meeting itself, we found that our vision aligned closely. As experienced entrepreneurs themselves, they understood the importance of unit economics and the business model. By the end of another couple of follow-up meetings, we seemed to speak the same language in terms of our approach to business. And most importantly, we seemed to share a passion for bringing ethnic foods to every doorstep.

Craftsvilla saw a natural alignment of our platform with their overall strategy of being market leaders of ethnic Indian products across categories. They wanted to acquire our business. However, we had never anticipated or considered acquisition as an option at this early stage!

Sudarsan and I had many passionate discussions. We chose to take the unconventional route and went ahead to negotiate the offer. From the very start, our dream was always to translate our idea into a viable business that delivered real value for food lovers and producers. The nitty-gritty of fundraising and ownership structures were only going to be the means towards this end.

Although unconventional, the acquisition option allowed us the freedom to continue to build our concept and move further towards our vision. We could see our happiness in being able to focus on building PlaceofOrigin.

Of course, we accept that circumstances and people will change with the passage of time. But given our objectives, circumstances and constraints in February 2016, we believe this was the right option, and we haven't looked back ever since.

Whether it is fund raising or acquisition, it is important to stay true and focused on your vision. And whatever be the offer on the table, it always comes with an associated philosophy. Therefore, it is equally important to align your vision and approach to business with that of your investor. If you are able to find that intersection of vision and approach within the constraints of your circumstances, that's when you know the offer is right for you to go ahead. Listen to your gut instincts.

People and circumstances will change, and you can't always pre-empt them. However, as long as your intentions are right, the outcome will be good.

PEOPLE SYSTEMS

It is important to ensure that the core team is functionally comprehensive in terms of the skill sets needed for product design, customer delivery, sales, finance and backend operations.

Often, a core team of two to five persons comes together to build a business based on their common vision. They could be driven either by their own aspirations or by market opportunity. It is important to have a founders' agreement to ensure alignment of the business goals with the personal aspirations of the core team and to define the rules of engagement and disengagement to avoid any heartburn later.

A bigger challenge arises when the team expands beyond the core team. Usually, members of the core team already have established personal relationships among themselves, having perhaps known each other for a long time. This allows many decisions and work tasks to be handled in an informal fashion with a give/take policy. When the team expands beyond the core group, interpersonal relationships become more professional and call for a formal engagement model for work allocation and decision making. Career growth, social identity, learning and earning potential are some of the key factors to consider for this extended team. It is, therefore, important to agree on broad roles and responsibilities for everyone, with associated work-flow and decision-flow procedures.

The inflection point at which to consider formalization of the engagement model for extended team collaboration can lie anywhere between a team size of five and twenty-five. It is typical to recruit experienced people for different functional areas. The extended team, along with the founding team, becomes the backbone of the firm for scaling the business.

Any human resources in addition to this extended team typically consist of employees recruited for scaling skillsets. These hires may be more tuned towards employment security and learning opportunity. The persons in the extended team segment have usually sacrificed their lifestyle, job security and income level in joining the firm and, hence, expect a career-enhancing title, a non-linear earning structure and a meatier role in the organization.

A rush for full-stack developers

1. Design and Production Process Models

Most design and production models involve an early market validation of the product or service after the concept is proven. A variant of an 'Agile' process model with a two-week or four-week cycle is typical.

It is important to differentiate a lab model from a production model. As the resource levels are highly optimized in a start-up, it is typical to have both the types of tasks performed by the same team members.

As the system scales, it is good to keep separate teams for these functions to avoid the experimental assets getting mixed up with the production assets. It is also important to isolate the customer-facing teams (who have customer data) from the lab teams (who have experimental data) to avoid any cross-flow of data and programmes.

2. Financial Models

It is critical to define the revenue model for the firm. Often, the users are not the payers in the business, and it is important to specify what is getting billed to the customer. In other words, the billing unit needs to be defined. The costs that are customer-centric need to be separated from the costs of the common product or of service development.

It is advisable to keep a check on the market numbers for Gross Profit Margin (GPM) and Earnings Before Interest, Taxes, Depreciation and Amortization (EBITDA) to decide where the firm needs to pay and why. For B2B start-ups, which have long sales cycles, it is also important to focus on working capital management to avoid running out of cash.

3. Site Operations

Most start-ups operate out of a single site in terms of physical location and may have other points of presence for customer access. It is important to restrict the number of sites to a few, because of the higher overhead costs associated with multiple sites. However, it is critical to have a physical location for the office so that the teams may visit each other for collaboration.

For online collaboration, there are many tools available such as Slack, Basecamp and Bluejeans.

It is essential to keep the domain name common (for websites, email IDs, etc.) for all team members, as well as for social, professional and organizational identity. Rarely do contracts for business allow information to be sent to anyone who does not have the domain name, unless a formal engagement document provides for it.

PROMOTER SPEAK

People Systems

Choosing a Culture Paradigm

Abir Barua, people orchestrator, Crayon Data

In one of our first early coffee-table gatherings at Crayon, we quickly came to realize that we were setting out to solve a huge problem that had not been tackled. It would have to be a unique blend of three different beasts: analytics, media and IT. It would take an eclectic bunch of people who would have to trust each other to bring together their own unique skills and perspectives in an unknown, untried way.

Right from the beginning we were sure about one thing: that the people we wanted and the culture we wanted to build, like everything else at Crayon, would have to be created, and we encapsulated them in a set of values we believed in very strongly:

1. *The mission is the boss*: Whoever in Crayon had the knowledge to lead the task was given the mandate to lead. This was regardless of seniority or experience.

2. *We hire people, not roles*: We always looked at the person first, regardless of his skills and expertise. Our interview process required the person to meet as many people in Crayon as possible, not just the people he or she would work with. Each interview carried equal weight.

3. *Lead by power of attitude, not seniority; we have no hierarchy*: We had no titles, and people could give themselves whatever title they wanted. Internally we had role descriptions like Orchestrators, Transformers and Contributors.

4. *Democracy in strategy, and dictatorship in execution*: Anybody could sit in at any strategy meeting without an invitation and give his or her opinion, but ultimately we were all judged on how we delivered on our mission. Our evaluation process reflected this. People were asked to list down their achievements for the year. They rated themselves on effort and output. All the people in the team also gave individual ratings. This was aggregated and became the basis for the evaluation.

5. *Self-management*: With flexibility to determine their own schedule, we allowed people to work from home one day a week but they were also required to be responsive and connected at all times.

6. *Freedom to fail*: People were allowed to try out new things without fear of failure, as long as they learned something from it.

The result was that the environment in Crayon was chaotic, and to survive people had to embrace and navigate this chaos. When you are trying to solve a problem that no one has solved, you will need a mix of right- and left-brained people. You will have to allow for a potent mix of opinions, styles and intellectual freedom, which will lead to a certain amount of chaos—don't resist it, let it be.

However, this means that people you hire need to be mature and capable of receiving brutal feedback. Also, with great freedom comes great responsibility. Make sure that all the people responsible for making hires know how to asses people for these critical traits of maturity and responsibility.

Walk the walk. Your evaluation system must reflect your values. Reward the people who live up to your values and make it transparent.

PREVENTION OF SEXUAL HARASSMENT (POSH) ACT AND CASE STUDIES

- The POSH Act confers protection on all women at a workplace, irrespective of whether they are employees or not (contract workers, trainees, apprentices included). *'Workplace' includes (i) any department, organization, undertaking, establishment, enterprise, institution, office, branch or unit which is established, owned, controlled or wholly or substantially financed by funds provided directly or indirectly by the appropriate Government or the local authority or a Government company or a corporation or a co-operative society; (ii) any private sector organization or a private venture, undertaking, enterprise, institution, establishment, society, trust, non-governmental organization, unit or service provider carrying on commercial, professional, vocational, educational, entertainment, industrial, health services or financial activities including production, supply, sale, distribution or service; (iii) hospitals or nursing homes; (iv) any sports institute, stadium, sports complex or competition or games venue, whether residential or not, used*

106

for training, sports or other activities relating thereto; (v) any place visited by the employee arising out of or during the course of employment including transportation provided by the employer for undertaking such journey; (vi) a dwelling place or a house. Given the objective of the act and the definition of workplace, this should also include digital workplace.

- It only applies to women and is not gender neutral.
- Unwelcome acts of behaviour are (whether directly or by implication):

    a) physical contact and advances;
    b) a demand or request for sexual favours;
    c) sexually coloured remarks;
    d) showing pornography;
    e) any other unwelcome physical, verbal or non-verbal conduct of sexual nature.

- The following acts may also amount to sexual harassment, if they occur in relation to a sexual act or behaviour:

    a) implied or explicit promise of preferential treatment;
    b) threat to employment prospects;
    c) creation of intimidating, offensive or hostile work environment;
    d) humiliating treatment, which can affect the victim's health or safety.

- The scope of 'workplace' is also extensive, and includes branches, any place visited by an employee (client office, for instance), office vehicles, etc.
- An Internal Complaints Committee (ICC) has to be constituted by all employers who have ten or more

employees, and any complaints can be brought to the ICC by an aggrieved person/relative/coworker/any person having knowledge of the incident.

- Complaints have to be made within three months of an incident; and within six months in grave circumstances, which have to be proved.
- The complainant must check with ICC on the procedure at the time of making a complaint. No lawyers are allowed. But ICC will function like a court.
- The aggrieved person and the accused can agree to a settlement with ICC's mediation, but there can be no monetary settlement.
- During proceedings, interim relief by way of transfer or leave can be granted.
- Punishment can include warning or reprimand, withholding of promotions, pay rises or increments, deduction of penalty or compensation from wages, termination of employment, etc.
- The aggrieved person or employer can also report the incident to the police. If the complaint is false or the witness statements are false, ICC can take action against the complainant or the witness. But mere lack of evidence is not reason enough to take action against them.

Case 1:

Situation: Employee A was working in an MNC in a mid-senior-level position. During the increment award period at the firm, she accused her immediate boss of discriminating against her on the basis of her gender and said she was not given the compensation she deserved. In her opinion, other tefam members who were not worthy of high increments were offered more than they deserved.

A complaint was filed with the Internal Complaints Committee (ICC) of the firm.

Complaint: As employee A believed she was discriminated against on the basis of her gender and was not offered an increment proportionate to her capability, she invoked her fundamental right to equality and right to life, guaranteed under Articles 14, 15 and 21 of the Constitution of India, and stated that the same were violated.

Outcome: The ICC looked into the matter at length and inquired as to the details pertaining to the complainant's punctuality, regularity and output. It was decided that the entire framework of appraisal should be revised, as what had happened amounted to 'indirect' non-verbal conduct that impeded the complainant's ability to deliver.

Case 2:

Situation: Employee X was on an official trip with her manager. At the hotel where they stayed, her room was right next door to the manager's. Employee X received a post-dinner call from the manager, who persistently tried, in many different ways, to have her come over for drinks at his hotel space. Employee X tried to dodge the invitation, implying her disapproval of it. The manager responded in a manner that implied that if she failed to go to his room it would lead to a downfall in her career.

Complaint: Employee X filed a complaint with the Internal Complaints Committee describing the manager's behaviour as being 'offensive, leading to a hostile working environment.'

Outcome: The burden was on the ICC to decide whether the harassment suffered by employee X was sufficiently severe to have created a hostile working environment. The manager was issued a notice leading to his termination, as the Committee was of the opinion that such an act as was committed by him amounts to 'sexual harassment', keeping in view the facts and circumstances.

Case 3:

Situation: The complainant was a 'contract employee' in the facilities team of an organization, with the role of overviewing cleanliness at the office space. It was alleged that one of her co-workers (who was also a contract employee) left her mortified with his unwelcome comments about her body type, resulting in the woman employee feeling embarrassed and being unable to work.

Complaint: The complainant approached the ICC to look into the matter and take a decision. She alleged that she was humiliated, which is 'inherently offensive', and constitutes sexual harassment.

Outcome: The ICC was of the view that it is important to check what determines and what constitutes 'sexual harassment'. The accused was terminated with immediate effect in order to maintain the sanctity of the workspace and the company's adherence to the POSH Act in its true spirit.

Case 4

Situation: The complainant said her team lead criticized the outfit she wore to the workplace, calling it 'inappropriate dressing for office'. She was told that her western partywear dress did not fit in the 'formal' or 'business formal' category. The team lead was of the view that such an outfit was inappropriate for office, and the complainant's colleagues too were of the same opinion. The complaint was in fact raised by the colleagues, following which the team lead had to intervene and educate the complainant on appropriate dressing. The team lead's questioning of her choice of dress was taken by the complainant as a personal insult.

Complaint: The complainant was furious with the warning letter issued by team lead and directly approached the HR lead. She did not consider it apt to settle the issue with the team lead, whom she intended to teach a lesson. To be taught by others how to dress was a violation of the 'right to life', said the complainant.

Outcome: As the complaint was filed under the POSH Act, the ICC had to intervene. It was unanimously decided by the committee that the warning issued to the complainant did not amount to a breach of the POSH Act. The objective of such a warning letter issued by team lead was to ensure that all the team members dressed to match the standards of the organization and in no event demeaned the values of the organization. The ICC also specified instances where the POSH Act comes to the rescue of aggrieved persons, and explained that this Act should not be misinterpreted or the platform misused.

THE LIFE STAGES OF
A START-UP AND KEY
ACTIVITIES AT EACH STAGE

An interesting and useful way to visualize a start-up is to see it in terms of life stages, just as one would the life of a human being.

The focus of this manual is to cover the aspects of a start-up during its first three years in human life cycle terms, from the time it is 'born' to the time it grows past the 'toddler' stage.

Stage 1: Newborn Phase (0–6 months)

– Idea formation
– Idea validation
– Core team setup
– Entity creation
– Proof of concept creation

Stage 2: Infancy Phase (6–12 months)

– Office setup

- Proof of concept validation
- Seed funding
- Initial or lead customer sign-up

Stage 3: Baby-steps Phase (12–18 months)

- Creation of business value proof points
- Reframing of value proposition and product features based on initial feedback
- Team expansion
- Partnerships creation
- Initiation of angel or institutional round

Stage 4: Stand-up Phase (18–24 months)

- Revenue scaling by increasing customer base
- Product hardening for robustness
- Setup of organizational processes and functions

Stage 5: Walk-ahead Phase (24–36 months)

- Raising of series A funds
- Creation of new product variants for scaling the footprint
- Geographical expansion

S01: Newborn Phase (0–6 months)

EN-01 Regulatory Checklist
EN-02 Accelerator Agreement
PP-01 Founders' Agreement
PP-02 Employee Agreement
PP-03 Adviser Agreement

PD-01 Business Plan Template

S02: Infancy Phase (6–12 months)

FN-01 Seed Investor Agreement and Cap Table
CS-01 Master Business Agreement—Customer
CS-02 B2C Experiments
CS-03 B2B First Order
PP-04 Team Recruitment beyond Core Team
PD-02 Product Strategy and Roadmap
PD-03 IPR-related Forms
PD-04 Product Sales Plan
MK-01 Marketing Plan

S03: Baby-steps phase (12–18 months)

FN-02 Institutional Investor Term Sheet
FN-03 Budgeting and Financial Plans
FN-04 Investor Reporting
PP-04 ESOP Agreement
PP-05 Performance Management and Benefits Plan
EN-06 Partnership Agreement
EN-07 Main Site Office Agreement
EN-08 New Office-in-a-Region Agreement
MK-02 Business Agent Agreement
CS-02 Maintenance and Support Agreement

S04: Stand-up Phase (18–24 months)

PD-05 Product Architecture and Performance
MK-03 Competition Metrics and Benchmarks
MK-04 Market/Media Analyst Sign-up Sheet

EN-06 Quality Process Plan
EN-07 Information Security Policy and Plan
FN-05 Bridge-Round Term Sheet/Convertible Note
FN-06 Positive or Breakeven Economics

S05: Walk-ahead Phase (24–36 months)

PD-06 Product/Platform Variants Plan for Scaling
FN-07 Series A Term Sheet

Document Keys

PD: Product
EN: Entity
FN: Finance
PP: People
CS: Customer
MK: Market

TEMPLATE EN-02:

ACCELERATOR AGREEMENT

S. No.	Checklist Item
1	Registered Company Name
2	Registered Address of the Company
3	Date of Incorporation of the Company
4	Main activities of the company as per the MoA of the Company
5	Copy of Incorporation Certificate
6	Copy of PAN Card of the Company
7	Copy of TAN Card of the Company
8	Copy of GST Registration Certificate of the Company
9	Copy of Professional Tax Registration Certificate as Business Entity
10	Copy of Professional Tax Registration Certificate as Employer (if applicable)

11	Copy of Shops and Establishments Registration Certificate
12	Copy of Resolutions passed at the first Board Meeting of the Company (certified by a director)
13	Copy of form ADT-1 filed for appointment of the Statutory Auditor in the first Board Meeting and the corresponding Receipt evidencing filing
14	Form MGT 14 filed for Resolutions passed at the first Board Meeting of the Company (certified by a director) (if applicable)
15	List of present Directors of the Company
16	Copy of Share Certificates issued for allotment of shares
17	Has the Company raised external funding? Please provide the details and the relevant agreements.
18	Details related to registration of Trade Mark/ Copy Rights/IP Rights (if applicable)
19	Copy of Bank Statement from Incorporation till date
20	The present shareholding pattern of the Company
21	Has the Company registered with DIPP as a start-up? If yes, please provide copy of Registration Certificate.

Key Points Related to GST for Start-Ups

The Goods and Services Tax (GST) has in many ways been a game changer. It has helped solve many issues related to multiple taxation on goods and services, but whether it is the 'panacea' we were longing for remains debatable. Start-ups, like many businesses, are affected by GST. There are a few important points to keep in mind when GST is implemented in the context of an early-stage start-up.

1. Registration under the GST regime is simpler than under the earlier tax regime. It is online and the entire process takes between three and seven days. This timeline is bound to reduce in the coming days.
2. While it is well known that the threshold limit is now Rs 40 lakh, it is important to note that this enhanced limit only applies to suppliers of goods. Most start-ups provide services, and the threshold for them remains Rs 20 lakh.
3. It is also important to know that the threshold limit is irrelevant if the start-up is engaged in exports. Registration becomes mandatory from Re 1. Once registration has been obtained and even supply made, even if turnover is below Rs 20 lakh or Rs 40 lakh, the business will attract GST.
4. The same principle applies when a start-up is an e-commerce platform or supplies through an e-commerce platform. If we consider services, then this would mean an 18 per cent tax outflow, and thus it is important for start-ups to price their products/services keeping the above principle in mind.
5. Filing GST returns has been made simple and it will continue to become simpler. Start-ups can opt for quarterly filing of certain returns instead of filing them on monthly basis. This will ease the compliance burden. Further, small businesses are exempted from filing of annual returns, and completely exempted from audit if their turnover is less than Rs 2 crore.
6. Are there any exemptions available to start-ups? Yes. There are. The incubatees located within a Technology Business Incubator or Science and Technology Entrepreneurship

Park recognized by the National Science and Technology Entrepreneurship Development Board (NSTEDB) enjoy exemption of GST for turnover of up to Rs 50 lakh. This means the start-ups need not charge any GST on their supplies. While the idea is to enhance their competitive pricing advantage, this exemption may not really help the start-up, for two reasons. The start-up will still need to pay GST on its purchases, and given that its supplies are exempt it will not be entitled to claim offset or refund of the taxes so paid. Competitive price advantage can still be achieved if the start-up's customer can claim input tax credit. Thus, it is immaterial for such a start-up whether the invoice includes GST or not.

7. Import of services attracts GST on 'reverse charge' basis. Many a time this is overlooked. Start-ups import many services into India and have to ensure that GST is duly paid on such import purchases. Of course, where eligible, the start-up can claim input tax credit of the GST so paid.

There are instances where firms show turnovers on their books that are different from the numbers on their GST returns. Start-ups tend to book GMV as their turnover – this helps them from an investment and valuation standpoint. However, in GST, only net income earned has to be disclosed. The two numbers have to be reconciled at the time of filing annual returns. Another pitfall is to not apply the correct rate. Given that most start-ups quote a 'tax-inclusive' price, incorrect rates would end up eating into their thin margins. If the price is inclusive of GST, the net amount is computed by eliminating the tax component and if that amount is more than 2Crores, then the entity is subject to GST audit.

Start-ups also incorrectly consider coverage under the Composition Scheme, which is quite restrictive and availably mostly for goods. Finally, due care has to be given to payments and the tax heads under which payments are made; incorrect payments will lead to locking up of funds till they are refunded by the department.

In a typical accelerator agreement, the accelerator operator agrees to provide several services to selected young companies/entrepreneurs. As a rule, accelerators run their programme at specific time intervals for batches or groups of companies admitted into their programme. Typically, while individuals are admitted into accelerator programmes, there is usually a requirement that a company be incorporated to receive financial grants or early investments.

The services provided by accelerators can be broadly classified as common or selective services. There is no fixed formula, but there appears to be some services or facilities common to all participants in accelerator programmes ('common services') and a few services or facilities selectively offered to participants at the discretion of the accelerator operator. The focus of this note is to provide a brief introduction to the 'common services' offered in the accelerator agreement.

1. Typical Common Services and Clauses

Use of physical space: One of the key offers made by the accelerator to the start-up is the right to use a specific physical space for a period of time. The space will be provided on a shared or co-working basis, i.e., all the participants in a specific batch at an accelerator will share the workspace, each participant usually allotted a specific designated work station or space for regular activities such as coding or preparing materials, and offered access to conference rooms and reprographic facilities on a shared basis. Co-location or co-working is a key attribute of accelerator programmes, and therefore, accelerator agreements often contain detailed clauses on use of specifically assigned as well as common areas.

Use of virtual resources: Another key accelerator offer is the use of virtual resources such as Internet connectivity, networking and sometimes even facilities for demonstrations and tests. These facilities are usually provided on a shared basis, and accelerator agreements should have very specific clauses on how they can be used. For example, it may be prohibited to run applications that completely consume the networking bandwidth during normal work hours. There will almost always be restrictions on what constitutes acceptable use of Internet connectivity.

Access to mentors/shared services: Accelerators typically have focus areas and build relationships with experts in these areas of focus. They may subsidize or offer free access to key services, such as financial or legal, from these experts. This is a key value-add offered by accelerators, but usually, the agreement will make it clear that these advisory services are on a no-commitment basis and that neither the accelerator nor the mentor will take on any liability for advice provided to the participant. Some accelerator agreements may require that participants work very closely with their assigned mentors to validate or refine their ideas, but even in such cases, it will be rare for the mentor or the accelerator to assume any responsibility or liability for outcomes.

No liability for outcomes: As already discussed in the previous point, accelerator agreements will usual disclaim all responsibility for outcomes resulting from an entrepreneur's or entity's participation in an accelerator programme. Young companies need to understand this. While it is an advantage if an accelerator validates an idea or offering by making additional services or seed investment available, many accelerator participants will not be offered such validation and will not have any recourse to the accelerator if their failure to obtain validation has an adverse impact on the viability of their company or its offering.

List of responsibilities: Accelerator agreements will contain a list of responsibilities that each participant will need to comply with while enrolled in the accelerator programme. This may encompass requirements relating to usage of facilities, access to facilities, compliance with codes of conduct, and requirements regarding compliance with the applicable laws.

Limited period: An accelerator programme will come to an end after a finite period as specified in the agreement. The duration of the programme varies from accelerator to accelerator, but it is reasonable to except a minimum term of ten to twelve weeks. In areas where it takes longer to develop proof of concept, the term is likely to be longer. All the participants in a batch will be required to vacate the facilities at the end of the programme for the batch, unless a specific exemption is made.

Investment: Some accelerators assess the performance of participants during the programme, after which they offer a small investment or grant to selected participants on pre-fixed terms, providing the participant with some initial money to further develop his/her idea/project after the programme. If this injection of money is structured as an investment, the accelerator operator will get shares in the company in return for the money. If it is a grant, then it is usually not linked to the issuance of shares, but the accelerator operator may ask for special rights to participate in future share issues by the participant at discounted terms. The accelerator operators use the appreciation in their equity investments as their primary route to fund the accelerator. Accelerators funded by large companies are more likely to make grants instead of investments, since their motivation in running the accelerator is to access cutting edge developments in their areas of interest, as opposed to seeing the accelerator as an income generator.

Consideration: Certain accelerators that operate on a commercial basis may require the participants to pay a sum of money, usually small, towards the services provided. This money may come out of the initial investment offered by the accelerator operator. Other accelerators prefer to rely on other forms of consideration, such as capital appreciation or preferential access to new developments.

Confidentiality: Accelerator agreements provide for very limited confidentiality protection. This is because like venture capital firms, accelerators too, especially if they have a specific area of focus, consider many entrepreneurs developing similar ideas. Accelerator operators will be very reluctant to commit to strict confidentiality, since they want to freely engage with companies and entrepreneurs without having to worry about what they say or do.

Intellectual property: Most accelerators clearly state that IP created by a participant belongs to the participant. The accelerator may also allow participants to license IP from it/ third-party licensors.

In addition to these subjects, standard representations, warranties and other boiler plate clauses are typical to all accelerator agreements of a similar nature.

TEMPLATE PP-01:

FOUNDERS' AGREEMENT

1. Introduction

This agreement is entered into by the promoters/founders of a company. It is essential to record the mutual understanding between the co-founders regarding the functioning of the company and their obligations towards the other co-founders as well as towards the company to mitigate complications and 'what if' situations that may arise in the future. However, a founders' agreement can be more than just a fail-safe measure and should be used as a guide recording the equity structure, business plan, roles and responsibilities, decision-making mechanism, management of operations, etc., of the company. While a founders' agreement can be finalized at any stage, the ideal time for it is as early as the pre-incorporation stage.

The key terms of a founders' agreement are as follows:

Initial investment, equity structure and ownership, and further investment: This provision is to record the investment or contribution of each co-founder and the percentage of shares held by each. Their contribution can be equal or unequal, financial (initial capital contribution) or in kind, or in the nature of time, effort, experience, expertise, knowledge, network, credibility, technical and managerial skills, and reputation. Thus, recording the split and allocation of equity ownership among the founders is imperative to avoid future conflicts.

The provision may also make allowance for future investment by third parties and/or impose an anti-dilution right, which ensures that any further issue of shares does not affect the percentage of shareholding of the co-founders.

Roles and responsibilities: This provision elaborates the role and responsibilities of each founder. While founders may prefer to have broad roles and make collective decisions, this might become paralysing and impractical with time, as the company grows. Thus, it is important to designate the more significant role that each co-founder plays and list down the services offered by each to the company. Recognizing the roles and responsibilities in writing ensures accountability and minimizes miscommunication and future conflicts.

However, allocation of designation should not lead to co-founders making unilateral decisions without consulting with other co-founders, as this can lead to erosion of trust. The key here is to establish clear areas of responsibility for each co-founder, specifying the type of decisions that require consultation, approval or unanimous consent. The provision should also allow for redefinition of roles as the responsibilities of the founders may change with the growth of the company.

Broad contours of business: This provision mainly defines the business or the potential venture of the company. It also describes the business plan and the milestones that need to be met by the company within specified time periods.

Compensation: This provision sets out the compensation structure with respect to the founders for the services they provide to the company. The compensation may be in cash or equity. Generally, a separate employment agreement is signed between the company and each individual founder detailing the terms of remuneration payable to him/her in lieu of his/her services.

Board representation and management: This provision specifies the constitution of the board, the procedure and quorum for board meetings and the voting rights of each co-founder. It deals with the appointment of the chairperson and the according of veto rights to him/her. As mentioned above, allocation of responsibilities among the co-founders invariably leads to delegation of decision-making authority. On the other hand, non-allocation of responsibilities and a purely collaborative way of functioning may lead to confusion and difficulty in decision making. Thus, it is essential to describe the manner in which various types of decisions will be made, specifying which items or matters may require consultation, approval, majority consent or unanimous consent.

Deadlock and resolution of deadlock: This provision is key to facilitating quick resolution of irreconcilable differences among the founders. A deadlock refers to a disagreement among the co-founders, wherein there are equal votes for and against and neither side is prepared to compromise. A deadlock could also arise if the founders are unable to reach unanimous consent on those items or matters that require it. The provision essentially defines what constitutes a deadlock and sets up a framework to resolve it in the most efficient and profitable manner.

Common deadlock resolution procedures include grant of casting vote to the chairperson of the board, use of an outsider's swing vote, reference to mediation, arbitration or expert determination, transfer of shares or, as a last resort, voluntary liquidation.

Exit notice: This provision clarifies the procedure for exit of a co-founder and requires the exiting co-founder to provide advance prior notice in writing to his co-founders and/or company in the agreed form and manner.

Lock-in, vesting and share transfer: In the nascent stages of the company, and at times even after, its success is heavily dependent on the co-founders and their contribution. Thus, it is important that a founder, from the point of view of the company and that of the remaining co-founders, continues to be associated with the company for a fixed period known as the lock-in period, during which shares held by him/her cannot be transferred. Accordingly, subject to negotiation between the parties, a founder may not be entitled to freely transfer his/her shares during the lock-in period.

The shares held by a founder may also be subject to periodic vesting as per a pre-determined vesting schedule. Upon expiry of the lock-in period, the founders may be subject to a specified share transfer or exit mechanism, such as a right of first refusal (ROFR) clause and a buy-back clause.

2. Promoter Covenants

Confidentiality: This provision essentially prevents the founders from disclosing, using or exploiting (unless required by law or by any regulation or by any governmental authorities or with proper authority) confidential information (as defined in the agreement) for any purpose. Further, the confidentiality obligation is generally perpetual in nature and ceases only when the information enters the public domain.

Non-solicitation: A non-solicitation provision prohibits the exiting co-founder from directly or indirectly engaging in business with the company's employees and/or customers against the interest of the company after his/her exit from the company.

Non-compete: This provision prohibits the co-founders from directly or indirectly being engaged or interested in any other company that competes against the start-up.

Intellectual property rights: The IPR provision provides clarity regarding ownership of information, inventions and discoveries developed, made or conceived by a co-founder, alone or jointly with others before, during or after incorporation of the company. All IPR developed by a founder in connection with the business of the company should ideally be assigned to and secured in the name of the company and not in the name of the specific co-founder who has developed the IPR. This is essential to ensure that the exit of a co-founder, such as the technical co-founder, does not affect the company's sole and unequivocal right over the IPR.

Term and termination: This provision stipulates the term of the founders' agreement, provided the agreement is for a fixed period. When a fixed term is mentioned, the agreement is automatically terminated on the expiry of that term. The provision also lists out the circumstances in which the agreement can be terminated before expiry of the term, such as voluntary or involuntary liquidation or breach of terms of the agreement, voluntary termination through unanimous consent of the founders, or death, incapacitation to work or insolvency of a co-founder. The provision may also list out the consequences of termination, post-termination obligations and post-termination asset distribution, as applicable.

Governing law and dispute resolution: This provision specifies the applicable substantive law, procedural law, place of jurisdiction and mode of dispute resolution.

TEMPLATE PP-02:

EMPLOYEE AGREEMENT

1. Employment Agreement for Key Employees

This agreement is used specifically for the hiring of executive employees performing functions that are core to the operation of the business of the company. The key employees may be either founders or promoters of the company who are also appointed as employees, or may be just employees holding such executive positions that are key to business operations. Due to the executive nature of this position, key employees fall outside the scope of the primary labour law legislations. Their service conditions are, therefore, governed by their respective employment agreements. The business relationship, rights, obligations, compensation structure, termination criteria and dispute resolution mechanism pertaining to them are solely contractual in nature.

The important terms of an employment agreement for key employees are as follows:

Terms and duties of employment or scope of employment: This provision lays down the designation, job description, duties and responsibilities of the key employee. The provision also recognizes the executive nature of the job, the continuous nature of obligations and, generally, restricts the key employee from engaging in any other business or enterprise without the prior permission of the company. It also demands that the company be informed regarding any such existing commitments.

Remuneration: The remuneration provision lays down the salary and other perquisites and benefits available to the key employee on fulfilment of obligations under the employee agreement. The remuneration and other perquisites/benefits generally covered in the provision are:

Salary: The definitive base salary payable in equal instalments at regular payment intervals during the term of employment is stipulated.

Benefits: The remuneration provision may refer to benefit plans (such as health or life insurance plans) available from the employer/company for the duration of employment.

Expenses: This provision reflects the reimbursement policy of the company, in effect from time to time. It may entitle the key employee to receive reimbursement for reasonable and customary business expenses incurred in the course of duty (such as travel expenses and hotel expenses).

Incentive compensation: Employers/company may choose to tie a portion of the key employee's compensation to the performance of the company to provide the key employee with an incentive to share and accomplish the company goals. The two common types of incentive compensation contained in key employment agreements are:

The bonus: Bonuses are a form of incentive compensation paid to the key employee as per the executive bonus plan of the company. Bonuses can be in the form of a sign-up bonus, a periodic or annual bonus, an incentive bonus or a discretionary bonus.

Stock options: Options to purchase shares of the company are granted to the key employees in accordance with the provisions of the stock option plan of the company. These stock options are periodically and/or conditionally vested, as per a pre-determined vesting schedule.

Confidentiality: This provision restricts a key employee from unauthorized use or disclosure of any confidential information and trade secrets that he/she receives or learns about while working for the company. Key employees form part of the core operations of the company, and thus, may have close knowledge of the confidential affairs of the company. The meaning of 'confidential information' is generally defined in the employment agreement. While the definition largely depends on the nature of the business of the company, the employer or company would want the definition to be broad and all-inclusive in scope, covering not only all kinds of company-related information but also third-party confidential information.

The key employee, on the other hand, would want a narrow definition of confidential information to limit his/her confidentiality obligations. This can be achieved by restricting the definition of 'confidential information' to information that is disclosed in writing (or oral disclosures reduced to writing) or information specifically marked as 'confidential' or specifying the information that is deemed confidential. It would also benefit the key employee to have certain exceptions made to the definition of confidential information.

The confidentiality provision may extend beyond the employee's term at the company. While the company may prefer to impose post-termination applicability of this provision, either for a fixed duration or in perpetuity, the key employee, naturally, will benefit from limiting this.

Intellectual property rights: The IPRs provision provides clarity regarding ownership of information, inventions and discoveries developed, made or conceived by the key employee, alone or jointly with others, during his/her term of employment with the company. Any such IPRs, as defined in the employment agreement, are generally considered 'work for hire', and the ownership of the same vests with the company. The provision may also require the key employee to irrevocably assign any IPR to the company and waive his/her enforcement right with respect to such IPR. The IPR provision subsists during the term of employment.

Non-solicitation: A non-solicitation provision prohibits the key employee from directly or indirectly engaging in business with the company's employees, customers (at times independent contractors such as suppliers) against the interest of the company for the duration of his/her employment and for a fixed period after termination of his/her employment with the company. The last restriction is due to access to the database (of customer/clients, commercials, employees, vendors, etc.) of the company that is made available to key employees, which constitutes confidential or proprietary information for the company. Non-solicitation restrictions are generally extended to the regular employees of the company too. To ensure that this provision is enforceable, it has to be framed in a reasonable manner in terms of scope and time period.

> *Note: Typically, the post-termination non-solicitation obligation may extend for a term ranging from six months to two years from the date of termination of employment.*

Non-compete: A non-compete provision prohibits the key employee from direct or indirect engagement with or interest in any business that competes against his/her employer during the course of employment and for a fixed period after his/her termination of employment with the company. It essentially protects the company against the possibility of an employee leaving the company and using his/her training, knowledge and contacts to the benefit of a competitor.

While a non-compete provision can impose an absolute or partial prohibition during the course of employment, its post-termination applicability may amount to a restraint on trade and, therefore, needs to be drafted carefully. The legal validity and enforceability of such a post-termination non-compete provision depends on the reasonableness of the provision in terms of time, geographical restrictions, scope of the non-compete and definition of competitor.

> *Note: Typically, in most key employment agreements, the post-termination non-compete obligation extends for a term ranging from six months to up to two years from the date of termination of employment. The investors generally prefer a*

broad definition of 'competitor', to include all such entities engaged in business similar to the company's. On the other hand, a narrow definition of the term that includes certain identified entities would be favourable to the founders/key employees.

Term and termination: This provision stipulates the term of the key employee's employment if it is for a fixed period. In case a fixed term is mentioned, the employment is subject to renewal by mutual consent of the parties upon expiry of the term. The provision also lists out the circumstances or grounds on which the employment can be terminated, either by the employer (company) or the key employee, before expiry of the term.

Termination by employer: Termination by the employer (company) can be with cause or without cause. The definition of 'cause' usually covers circumstances such as misconduct, non-performance and breach of terms of agreement. While companies may choose immediate termination in such circumstances, employees would benefit from a notice and cure provision, which allows them a fixed amount of time to cure the breach or problem.

While the company/employer would prefer a broad definition of 'cause', employees would benefit from a narrower definition as key employees are often entitled to stock options and severance payments, and may lose their eligibility for these benefits if they are terminated for a cause. Termination without cause would generally require the company to provide a prior written notice of one or two months (as agreed upon by the parties) or to pay salary to the key employee in lieu of the notice period.

Termination by employee: The key employee can also choose to resign and thus terminate his/her employment with the company at any time, with or without good reason. Since the employee is a key employee and is vested with significant responsibilities, he/she will generally be required to give notice and fulfil the notice period, unless the company agrees in writing to waive the notice period and instead, have the employee pay the company his/her salary in lieu of the notice period.

> **Note:** *Depending on the genus (including the founders' group) to which the key employee belongs, clauses relating to termination may be omitted for convenience or suitably drafted in line with the lock-in period (as detailed below) and the exit agreed upon with the investors. Longer notice periods may also be agreed upon, depending on the seniority of the employee and nature of the work in question.*

Governing law and dispute resolution: This provision specifies the applicable country law, place of jurisdiction and mode of dispute resolution in the event any dispute arises between the company and the key employee.

If the key employee is also a founder of the company, such employment might be subject to the following additional clause:

Lock-in period: The shares held by such a key employee (as referred to above) might be subjected to a lock-in. This essentially means that although the key employee already holds the shares, the same shall vest in his/her favour monthly, semi-annually or annually on a prorated basis for a fixed duration (as specified in the agreement) known as the vesting period. The exercisability and the vesting schedule of these shares are laid down in this provision.

This clause also provides for the status of vested and unvested shares in certain scenarios such as liquidation, change in control, termination of employment by company with or without cause, resignation by employee, or death or disability of the employee. Depending on the situation, the applicable law, the company policy and negotiations between the parties, the unvested option or shares may expire or be subjected to accelerated vesting, compulsory buyback or other similar modes of transfer/purchase as determined between the parties.

TEMPLATE PD-02:

IPR-RELATED FORMS

1. Confidentiality Undertaking (Sample)

> ### CONFIDENTIALITY/NON-DISCLOSURE UNDERTAKING FORMAT
>
> To,
> [NAME AND ADDRESS OF START-UP]
>
> This is in response to the letter of appointment for the post of _____, dated_____, issued to the undersigned by the [**START-UP**].
>   I shall be privy to information, documents, procedures, processes, products, technical dossiers, standards, test procedures and projects handled by me, as also of those under new product development. I am aware that all these are required to be kept highly confidential.

In this context, I hereby unequivocally undertake and assure you:

1. That I shall not reveal any project matters or those under development while I am in service/as a staff/contractor/consultant and after the term has ended for any reason whatsoever,
2. That I shall not act in a manner prejudicial to or damaging the interest of the START-UP at any time during my term/employment or thereafter,
3. That I shall not misuse any information relating to any subject matter for patenting or IPR or any other information during my tenure of service or after term end for any reason whatsoever,
4. I shall not use any proprietary information of START-UP for commercial use or industrial applications.

In the event of a breach of this undertaking and assurance in any manner whatsoever, START-UP shall be free to take any action as deemed fit and proper in law without any reference to me in the matter.

Yours faithfully,

_____

Name:
Designation:
Date:
Place:

2. Capturing Inventions (Sample)

INVENTION DISCLOSURE FORM

1) Title of invention:
2) Names and contact details of the Inventors:
3) Description of invention:
4) List of key elements of your invention that you consider novel and non-obvious:
5) Usefulness or advantage of your invention over pre-existing technology/solution:
6) List of relevant literature (patent/non-patent) or attachments that will help to distinguish the invention disclosure from the prior art (OPTIONAL):
7) Details of all public disclosure(s) related to the invention in exhibitions, seminars, conferences, or workshops by the inventor:
8) Any additional notes/comments:

TEMPLATE PP-03:

ADVISER AGREEMENT

1. Mentor/Adviser Agreement

A mentor/adviser agreement is between the adviser(s) and the company. The advisers may play a vital role in guiding a company on matters in which they have expertise and experience. Advisers do not form a part of the company's workforce, as they are not hired by the company as employees or consultants. Advisers are independent persons who provide advisory services to a company.

The compensation to advisers may be either in cash or equity. Generally, advisers are compensated with equity since it may be difficult for start-ups to spare cash to pay them. Also, equity-based incentive ensures that the advisers remain invested in the company. An adviser agreement is important for outlining the obligations of the adviser and formalizing the relationship between the adviser and the company.

The key terms of an adviser agreement are:

Services: This provision contains the list and nature of advisory services to be provided by the adviser. While not mandatory, and dependent on the nature and arrangement being sought from the adviser, the company may insist on a certain specified number of hours that an adviser is expected to dedicate to the company on a periodic basis. As mentors/advisers are not meant to function like employees or consultants and their services are rendered in good faith, this provision may not be included. In certain instances, instead of a specified number of hours, the company may mandate achievement of certain milestones to assess adviser contribution.

Compensation and release of shares: This provision sets out the compensation, and its scheduling, payable to the adviser for services rendered during the term of the agreement. As the compensation is usually in terms of equity in the company, the compensation clause includes a release schedule, i.e., the period at the end of which a certain percentage of the compensatory equity is released to the adviser.

> **Note:** *Typically, depending on the complexity of the advice being provided, the shares allocated towards the advisory pool may range from 1–4 per cent of the shareholding of the company.*

Term: The term or time period of the agreement may be determined depending on the nature of advice being provided by the adviser and the requirement of such advice by the company. For example, if the advice relates to the structuring of the business, the company may require it only during its initial phase; but if the advice is for operations, marketing, technology or networking, the company may need it for longer durations. Also, the term of an advisory agreement for milestone-linked advisory services may extend up to the time of achievement of the specified milestones.

Termination: The parties may agree on an initial lock-in period during which neither party is allowed to terminate the agreement. The termination clause is particularly important in an adviser agreement as it pertains to the treatment of released and un-released shares upon termination of the agreement. The company may require the adviser to sell back a certain portion of the released shares upon premature termination of the agreement. The treatment of shares will vary depending on the reason behind termination of the agreement, i.e., whether it was based on a cause (misconduct, conviction or breach of terms by adviser) or done for convenience.

Non-disclosure of confidential information: This clause restricts advisers from sharing confidential information of the company with a third party or for purposes other than the benefit of the company.

No conflicts: Mentor/advisory agreements generally do not contain anti-competitive restrictions. The mentors/advisers are generally members who have gained extensive expertise in a specific field. It may not be agreeable to advisers to be bound by anti-competitive restrictions as this may hinder them from using their expertise for other purposes. However, if the area of expertise of the adviser and the company is extremely narrow, it is advisable to carve out provisions that ensure there is no conflict of interest. Through this provision, the adviser represents and provides an undertaking to the company that his/her advisory services to the company does not result in any conflict of interest. The provision also obligates the adviser to notify the company if any conflict of interest occurs or is foreseen to occur in the near future. Upon such notification, the company reserves the right to decide whether to continue with the adviser or terminate the relationship.

Nature of relationship: This provision specifically states that the arrangement between the adviser and the company is on a principal-to-principal basis and that the adviser is *not* an employee of the company. The clause also states that the adviser shall not have any right or authority to enter into any contracts on behalf of the company.

Assignment of intellectual property: This provision is to determine that any information, inventions and discoveries developed, made or conceived by the adviser in the course of provision of advisory services shall be considered 'work made for hire' and all rights relating to such intellectual property shall belong to the company.

TEMPLATE MK01:

DIGITAL MARKETING PLAN

1. Digital Properties

The company blog

The start-up/promoters should set up a blog on WordPress, which is free and offers many amazing plugins. One can start by installing Yoast, an SEO plugin that will help Google and other search engines locate and rank one's content. (Other great plugins include Akismet, Calendar, and featured posts).

Once the back-end of the blog is ready to go, its curb appeal must be considered. How does the design look? A professional designer can be asked to help with the design. The blog should primarily be about publishing great content at the right time, pitched to the right people. Its design should simply enhance that experience.

The blog must have the following functionalities:

Blog subscription and RSS feed
Social sharing options
Search facility

Social media

They are among the most popular forums for a start-up to promote its content and reach influencers. Since a great content promotion plan brings potential customers to the start-up website, and since influencing the influencer can generate thousands of new leads, social media and its networks are invaluable to start-ups.

The right social media networks

Start-ups tend to choose the social media networks they engage on without much strategy.

Facebook, Twitter, LinkedIn, Tumblr, Reddit, Pinterest and, now, Instagram are some of the most popular social networks today. All of them can be great content promotion and community building tools but each has unique characteristics.

Each 'works' differently, in terms of how the community receives, interprets, digests and shares content on them. Therefore, one must be mindful of the network and community that is being targeted.

For a start-up in the B2B space, LinkedIn and Twitter are two channels that will prove most effective.

List of influencers

One of the best marketing techniques online is to influence the influencer. The influencer list must be built with a bit of market research. A good way to start is by finding popular blogs in the space. Who writes for those blogs? Who owns them? When searching for the start-up's core keywords on Twitter, who appears in the results? Whom are they following?

However, a high follower count is not always a good indicator of influence. How engaged an influencer's followers are, and their follower-to-following ratio, must be considered too. Klout Score can be used to measure their influence.

2. Public Relations

Identifying the right writers for the media list

The key media outlets must be first determined and then a search done for stories with themes relevant to the start-up. Who are the writers of those stories?

The start-up must always pitch its story to the right writer. Once the writers have been identified, social media must be used to connect with them. It is important to build relationships with the writers but to ask nothing of them. Private Twitter lists of writers of interest can be created, and their tweets actively responded to and retweeted. It is important to *make friends with them*!

Creating a press kit

The key to a successful media launch is rooted deep within a killer media kit. First comes identification of the required items, which include the following:

Media advisory
Logos and screenshots
Founder bios and photos

A media advisory should include all points that are important to the product, the company and its success. It should illustrate how the product/company is changing the world and why it is important.

Brief background information on the company and its founders should be included to offer a taste of the team behind the product. Quick stats at the end of the media advisory can provide snapshots of the company.

The handout must include:

- The company name
- Website
- Twitter handle(s)
- Names of CEO and co-founders
- Launch date (if applicable)

Reaching out to journalists

Engaging with journalists before one needs to reach out to them for something specific is key. When sending them information on a story that may interest them, it is proper to first ask them whether such information may be sent. As previously mentioned, by building a relationship first, a request to a journalist to consider a story possibility may not come off as insincere.

3. Content Creation

Creating a list of topics

Before diving right in to write, it is advisable to create a list of topics. The perfect topic list for SEO purposes should be based on the core keywords of the start-up. One way to start is by brainstorming ten topic ideas around each of the core keywords. Where possible, the keywords must be used in the titles of blog posts, but not in a way that they sound unnatural. The ideas must be put into a blog calendar that can help track posts from conception to completion.

Knowing what types of content to publish

There are five main types of content that can be published. These are blogs, eBooks, white papers, newsletters and videos.

Guest blogging

Promoters can start by looking for guest blogging opportunities at the top blogs that cater to their target market. Most blogs will openly accept guest posts, so one must look out for a writers' page or contributors' page. If this is not easy to do, the blog owner or editor can be tracked down on social media and requested to look at the draft of the promoter's blog post. The post should be of high quality and 100 per cent original.

Once the start-up promoter has built a reputation, it will be easier to find influencers willing to contribute to his start-up blog, where its own writers' page can be created and for which select influencers can be reached out to via social media or email. When the guest post is published, the contributor must be pinged so she can promote the post to her network.

Capturing emails

Email subscription has been mentioned a few times already. There are three routes to capturing emails: email submits, newsletter subscriptions and blog subscriptions. Email submits could come from downloads of free eBooks or similar offers. Newsletter subscriptions are just that: people interested in reading regular updates and content from the start-up. Blog subscriptions are straightforward too.

Email submits and newsletter subscriptions are best managed by tools like MailChimp, which allows the easy sending of well-designed custom emails to leads. Blog subscriptions are best managed by tools like Feedburner, which allows automatic notification of leads when new blog content is published.

4. Events

Events can be a bit of a black hole if not analysed and decided upon well. They are a great way to reach out to prospects, build a lead list and to showcase products. However, quality and audience checks are key. Events could be a great way to enter the markets being targeted. Pre-event and post-event outreaches are very important. *An event is only as good as its follow-up.*

While creating a calendar of events across geographies and verticals, the following criteria must be kept in mind: Does the event cater to prospects in focus geographies and focus verticals?

Is there a good value-proposition and product that is ready to scale to showcase?

Is every event the best for the vertical in question for that quarter and the next?

Is a sales team/consultant/partnership in place to pursue leads?

Is it primarily a brand-building event or a lead-generation event?

5. Marketing Tools and Technology

Setting up analytics tools

The key to measuring success is a great analytics tool. For a free solution, it is worth checking out Google Analytics. It provides the basics, and over time, the somewhat complicated behind-the-scenes mechanics of it can be mastered. There are also more user-friendly and advanced analytics tools available.

The experience of setting up one's analytics tool will vary depending on the solution chosen. However, all analytics tools will have one insert a snippet of code in one's web pages, which allows the tools to track visits and events. One must make sure to look for analytics tools that are committed to preserving fast load times.

Tools to automate social media

Keeping up with emerging social media networks is challenging. There are tools like Hootsuite or Buffer that can be used to schedule social media updates. To follow relevant people and identify influencers, tools such as Crowdfire and FollowerWonk may be used. The good news is that these tools are free.

Email marketing

This is a cost-effective way to nurture new leads and stay engaged with existing customers. While there are many low-cost email marketing tools such as Get Response and Campaign Monitor, MailChimp is the only free one with a great set of features.

MailChimp is an email marketing tool that is free up to 500 contacts, which makes it perfect for small companies or start-ups. Despite being free, it still has powerful features that most paid email marketing tools have, such as tracking opens, clicks and bounces. On upgrading the service, access to marketing automation tools is available too.

Search engine optimization tools

There are hundreds of factors that go into Google's search result rankings. Here are some tools that can help one's website and content perform better when it comes to user experience and quality.

Google Keyword Planner

This shows the search volumes per month of search terms provided by the start-up, and the search volumes for related terms too. This tool can also generate a list of keywords based on the URL that one submits. Understanding how often keywords are searched on Google can help the start-up prioritize and brainstorm blog-post ideas and see what types of searches are most in demand.

Google Mobile-Friendly Test

As of 21 April 2015, Google implemented changes to the mobile search rankings that favour mobile-friendly websites. Entering one's URL in this tool will show whether one's website is mobile-friendly or not. If the start-up site is not mobile-friendly, the tool sends suggestions for changes.

Google Webmasters

Google Search Console is a free service offered by Google that helps the monitoring and maintenance of a website's presence in Google Search results. The start-up does not have to sign up for Search Console for its site to be included in Google's search results, but doing so can help it understand how Google views its site and can help optimize its performance in search results.

6. Customer Relationship Management

A Customer Relationship Management (CRM) system tracks sales activities and customers. Having a tool and process to track potential deals is especially important to new businesses, which need to generate revenue. It may be tempting to just use an Excel spreadsheet to track sales activities, but a CRM is much better for tracking.

Hubspot CRM

Hubspot's CRM is free, modern and easy to use. The dashboards can display where different deals are in the sales cycle, show one's contacts and it can even integrate with Sidekick (also free), an email tracking app, to automatically add emails sent to the CRM.

Insightly

This is another free CRM that is relatively easy to use and integrates with other marketing tools such as Gmail and MailChimp.

TEMPLATE FN-01:

SEED INVESTOR AGREEMENT

1. Term Sheet

Companies raise funds from external investors at various points during the life cycle of their business.

The process of raising funds starts with the founders of the company pitching their idea and describing the product to probable investors. If an investor seems interested, the investor(s) and the founders (called the 'parties') execute a 'term sheet', which is a non-binding document that broadly captures the high-level understanding between the parties with regard to the terms of the proposed investment. If the parties agree on the terms under the term sheet, the investor(s) may conduct due diligence exercises on various aspects of the operations of the company.

Subject to the outcome of these exercises, the parties initiate the drafting and finalization of the legal documents, primarily the share subscription agreement and the shareholders' agreement. These agreements are often highly negotiated, and elaborately capture the terms of the proposed investment.

Some of the common terms and conditions in a term sheet touch upon the following:

Nature of securities to be issued by the company: Under the Companies Act, 2013, a company in India can issue the following types of securities that will determine the interest of the security holder/investor in the company:

- Equity shares
- Compulsorily convertible preference shares
- Compulsorily convertible debentures

Equity shares are the fundamental shares of the company that give its holders a certain degree of control in the company. Preference shares and debentures, on the other hand, are convertible instruments[1] (convertible into equity shares of the company), the holders of which enjoy certain preferred rights in the company as against holders of equity shares. Depending on the nature of the instruments that the parties agree on, the consequent rights and obligations of the parties are determined and captured in the term sheet.[2]

---

[1] As per the provisions of applicable law, a company can issue convertible securities for a certain fixed tenure, at the end of which such instruments would have to be mandatorily converted into equity shares of the company. Accordingly, the Parties often determine the conversion ratio attached with the convertible securities. However, the same maybe subject to adjustments based on the performance of the company during the tenure of such convertible securities, and would be as per the provisions of the Companies Act as well as the applicable foreign exchange laws.

[2] Based on a valuation exercise that may be conducted, the investors and founders negotiate and determine the price of the securities of

> **Note:** *Typically, private equity funds and venture capitalists prefer compulsorily convertible preference shares. However, the preferred choice of securities for investors in the infrastructure, construction and housing sectors is compulsorily convertible debentures.*

Schedule of disbursement of investment amount: Subject to understanding between the parties, the entire investment amount may be remitted to the company in one tranche or in multiple tranches, often depending on certain performance-based milestones as may be agreed by the parties. The disbursement may also be linked to certain end-use restrictions, for example, the parties may agree that the funds being invested by a particular investor shall be deployed for certain specific needs of the company.

2. Control and Management[3]

Voting rights of shareholders: By subscribing to the shares (equity and preferential shares) of a company, the shareholders acquire voting rights in proportion to the percentage of their

---

the company that the investor will have to pay to subscribe to the desired securities of the company. The law surrounding the issue price of the shares vis-à-vis the valuation of the company is captured under the Companies Act as well as under the foreign exchange laws (with regard to the issue price of the shares of an Indian company by a non-resident investor).

[3] Depending on the nature and extent of rights that are extended to the investors, the charter documents of the company (articles of association and the memorandum of association) may be amended in order to incorporate the rights and restrictions as envisaged under the definitive agreements.

shareholding. This gives them the right to have a say in the management decisions and policies adopted by the company so that they can exercise due control on the functioning of the company to ensure protection of their investment.

Affirmative voting rights: While the founders of a company take the day-to-day operational decisions, investors are often extended affirmative voting rights regarding certain recognized matters as may be mutually agreed upon between the founders and investors. Such matters cannot be decided at a shareholder or board meeting without the express consent of the affirmative voting-right holders of the company.[4]

Board rights/observer rights: This clause includes the right of the investor to appoint a nominee on the board of directors of the company. The investor may also choose to nominate an observer, rather than a director, on the board of the company. However, the observer shall not have any voting rights in any business of the board.

> **Note:** *Typically, each investor is given one board seat. However, in case there are multiple small investors who have put in money, one investor from among them is appointed as the 'lead investor' who is given the right to appoint one or more directors on behalf of the other small investors.*

---

[4] Exercising of affirmative voting rights by the investor often leads to a deadlock between the parties. Accordingly, it is important to clearly draw out the manner of resolving deadlock between the investors and the founders in the definitive agreements (shareholders' agreement).

Liquidation preference:[5] This provision is about the mechanism of receipt of proceeds by shareholders (or different classes of shareholders) of the company in the event of liquidation or winding up of the company. Subject to applicable laws, certain shareholders of a company may have preferred contractual rights to receive the proceeds (up to an agreed amount) upon liquidation of the company. This liquidation may be of two types:

Participating liquidation reference: The surplus proceeds after payment to the preferred shareholders is distributed in a pro-rata manner among all the shareholders of the company, including the preferred shareholders; or

Non-participating liquidation preference: The surplus proceeds after payment to the preferred shareholders is distributed only among the remaining shareholders of the company.

> **Note:** *At the seed stage, the sector-agnostic liquidity preference of a participating nature is 1–1.5X. In the later stages, the liquidity preference in the IT sector may go up to 3X, non-participating. However, in rising sectors like education, manufacturing and energy, the liquidity preference in the growth stages is generally of a participating nature, and the threshold for the same may vary, subject to the agreement between the parties.*

---

[5] This provision is often suitably worded to include the mechanism of treatment of proceeds in cases of sale of the company, through merger, sale of shares, change in the control of the company or sale of the assets or undertaking of the company.

Anti-dilution adjustment: Early-stage investors in a company are exposed to fluctuations in the valuation of the company, against which investors often seek anti-dilution protection to prevent devaluation of the securities held by them. Accordingly, subsequent to investment by an investor, if the company issues new securities at a price less than what was paid by the investor, then the company shall be obliged to issue certain additional securities to the investor as may be determined by the following:

• The full ratchet mechanism
• The broad-based weighted average mechanism

> **Note:** *In the early stages of start-up funding in the country, when companies were solely driven by investments, the full ratchet mechanism was preferred for anti-dilution adjustment as this was more favourable to investors. However, in recent times, the broad-based weighted average mechanism has become the more popular choice of anti-dilution adjustment mechanism.*

Pre-emptive rights: Subject to negotiation between the parties, shareholders of a company often have a right to subscribe to additional shares of the company in the event the company issues new securities. The pre-emptive right of the shareholders shall be exercised simultaneous to the offer of new securities to the new shareholders.

Dividend: The quantum of dividend that may be declared is at the discretion of the board of the company. Dividends may be cumulative or non-cumulative; the first can be accumulated and carried forward to the succeeding year if unpaid in any year, but this is not possible with the second type.

Promoter lock-in, vesting, transfer rights:[6] It is an important consideration for an investor that the founders of the company continue to be associated with the firm until the exit of the investor or until the expiry of a period mutually agreed upon by the parties. To this end, investors propose and insist on incorporating certain provisions in the term sheet and in the shareholders' agreement.

Accordingly, subject to negotiation between the parties, a founder may not be entitled to freely transfer shares held by him throughout a lock-in period. The shares held by a founder or a key employee of the company may also be subject to periodic vesting, in accordance with a pre-determined vesting schedule.

Transfer restriction on shares of investor: This is subject to negotiation between the parties.

Exit rights: Financial investors intend to make profitable returns on their investment by selling their stakes in their investee company. Subject to negotiation between the parties, the term sheet may provide for specific mechanisms of exit to be followed by the company and the founders to give the investor the maximum profits possible. Such exits may be

---

[6] Subject to negotiation between the Parties, certain restrictions may also be imposed on the transferability of the shares/securities held by the investors to person or an entity engaged in competing business or to another investor whose interest might clash with that of the company.

through an initial public offering, buy-back of the investor's shares by the company, sale of the investor's shares to a third party, etc.

> **Note:** *It may be noticed that, of late, many transactions do not include an exit mechanism, which is left to the joint discretion of the parties. However, the parties generally pre-determine the period within which exit shall take place.*

Tag-along rights: The shareholder has the right to sell her shares along with another shareholder of the company selling his shares. A holder of the tag-along right is notified by the selling shareholder of the proposed sale and its details. The holder may choose to exercise her right and sell her shares in the company along with the selling shareholder, at the same price and on the same terms and conditions as the selling shareholder. If the proposed transferee refuses to buy all or part of the shares of the tag-along right holder, then the selling shareholder shall reduce proportionately the number of shares offered to be sold by him in order to accommodate the sale of the tag-along right holder's shares.

Drag-along right: Like the tag-along right discussed above, a shareholder may also have a drag-along right. Accordingly, in the event the investor is unable to secure an exit as per the option above, he may choose to exercise his drag-along right under which, subject to mutual agreement between the parties, he shall have the option to sell his shares to a third party and force the other shareholders to sell (either wholly or partly) too, if that will facilitate the sale.

Information/inspection rights: This clause states that the investors, upon request, shall have access to the books of the company for inspection.

Bridge round of funding: This is an additional round of funding raised by the company, prior to the series A round. The valuation for this round is either based on the then prevailing valuation of the company or can be done separately at the time of such funding. The terms of such a bridge round of funding are largely subject to the commercial understanding/ negotiation between the company and the bridge round investors, and are set out in a time-capped manner, i.e., subject to the raising of series A funds within a specified period.

One of the most integral terms usually incorporated in the bridge round term sheet is 'valuation adjustment'. Conversion of the convertible instruments, as proposed to be issued to the bridge round investors, is flexible and linked to the pre-money valuation of the company for a subsequent round of funding. In accordance with the commercial understanding between the parties, the bridge round investors may or may not be given a rebate on the price at which shares are proposed to be issued to subsequent investors.

Under an investment agreement for a bridge round, the section on valuation adjustment elaborates the various factors to be considered for conversion of any convertible instruments that may be issued to the bridge round investors. These factors include the following:

- The time or duration within which the adjustment may take place—a period anywhere between six and twenty-four months, depending on the general industry standards—and fund raising, as may be applicable to the specific sectors

- The ratio at which the instruments issued to the bridge round investors would convert
- The procedure for conversion of the convertible instrument into equity shares of the company

This clause also sets forth certain milestones in accordance with which conversion of the convertible instruments will be mandatory or optional, subject to the applicable conversion ratio and price at the time of such conversion. The bridge round term sheet takes into account the projected valuation (based on business plans, market practice, industry standards, etc.) at which a series A round of funding would be undertaken, to decide whether convertible instruments will be converted at a specified conversion price or at a discount to the conversion price arrived at during the series A round.

As per the applicable laws pertaining to any foreign direct investment in the company, it is pertinent to note that the price at which the shares of the company are valued in the valuation report should, at all times, be lower than the conversion price applicable at the time of conversion.

SAMPLE LIST OF INCUBATORS IN INDIA

S.No.	Name	Thrust Area	State	City	Address	Website Application Process	Apply Link	Contact Details
1	NASSCOM 10K Warehouse Vizag	Agnostic	Andhra Pradesh	Visakhapatnam	Sunrise Towers, Hill No. 3, ITSEZ, Madhurawada, Visakhapatnam, Andhra Pradesh	http://10000startups.com/startup-warehouse/		Vijay Kumar Bawra, Manager vijay@nasscom.in M: 9831524485
2	Agri Business Incubator	Agri-business	Andhra Pradesh	Patancheru	Agri Business Incubator International Crops Research Institute for the Semi-Arid Tropics ICRISAT, 303 Bldg, Patancheru -5023224	http://www.aipicrisat.org/	http://www.aipicrisat.org/join-us-2/	Dr Kiran Sharma, CEO k.sharma@cgiar T:: 040 3071 3300 /3417
4	IKP Knowledge Park Life Science Incubator	1) Life Science, 2) Medical Devices, 3) Materials	Andhra Pradesh	Secunderabad	Genome Valley, Turkapally, Shameerpet, Ranga Reddy Dist, Hyderabad 500 078	http://www.iikpknowledgepark.com/index.php	http://www.iikpknowledgepar k.com/par-of-ikp.php	Dr. Sangita Sen Majee, Head – Life Science Incubator sangita@ikpknowledgedpark.com Fax: 040 3071 3074/75

#	Name	Sector	State	City	Address	Website	Contact
5	IITG-Technology Incubation Centre (IITGTIC)	1) IT 2) Healthcare 3) Renewable energy 4) Mechanical	Assam	Guwahati	IITG-Technology Incubation Centre Technology Complex, IIT Guwahati Guwahati-781039 Assam, India	http://www.iitg.ac.in	Dr. J. K. Deka, Faculty In-Charge tic@iitg.ernet.in T: (0361) 2583191/2583194 Fax: 0361-2583195
6	Centre for Innovation Incubation and Entrepreneurship	Agnostic	Assam	Guwahati	Panikhati,down town hospital ltd, building#3, 7th floor, G.S.road, guwahati-6	https://adtu.in/	Mr. Joutishman Dutta, Principal jd@downtowngroup.org M: 9706011569
7	Bihar Entrepreneurs Association	Agnostic	Bihar	Patna	Enterprising Zone-EZ, aa 128/E, Opposite Children's Park, SK Puri, Boring Road, Patna-8000001	http://www.enterprisingzone.com	http://beabihar.com/ Submit-your-idea#BEA	Mr. Abhishek Kumar, BEA abhishek2709@gmail.com M: 09708899777 T: 0612-3222433
8	Bihar Industries Association	Agnostic	Bihar	Patna	Bihar Industries Association, Industry House, Sinha Library Road, Patna-800001	http://www.biabihar.com/	http://biaincubator/biaincubator/index.php/apply	Mr. Ram Lal Khaitan, BIA, hi.techpatna@gmail.com M: 09334145197 T: 0612-2226642/22221100/3260717

#	Name	Sector/Focus	State	City	Address	Website	Contact
9	Business Incubation Centre (IC)	1) Electronics System Design and manufacturing (ESDM) with a special focus on Medical Electronics	Bihar	Patna	Ground Floor, Administrative Block, IIT Patna campus, Bihta, Patna -801106. Bihar.	http://www.iciitp.com/	Aditya Nataraja, Manager sriru@iitp.ac.in T: +91-612-3028545/6/7
10	Foundation for Innovation and Technology Transfer, IIT Delhi	Science & Technology	Delhi	Delhi	Indian Institute of Technology, Delhi [IITD], Hauz Khas, New Delhi -110 016, INDIA	http://fitt-iitd.in/	Dr. Anil Wali, Managing Director 1) anilwali@fitt.iitd.ac.in 2) mdfitt@gmail.com T: 011-26857762
11	National Small Industries Corporation Limited	1) Energy 2) Pumps	Delhi	Delhi	NSIC Bhawan,Okhla Industrial Estate, New Delhi-110020	http://www.nsic.co.in/	Mr.Satvinder Singh, Senior General Manager 1) pkbiswas@gmail.com 2) gmtech@nsic.in T:# 011-26317482, Fax:011-26317482

| 12 | Shriram Institute for Industrial Research (A Unit of Shriram Scientific and Industrial Research Foundation) (www.shriaminstitute.org) | Multidimensional services in the manufacturing sector of Plastics, Rubbers, Specialty Chemicals and Waste Management | Delhi | Delhi | SHRIRAM INSTITUTE FOR INDUSTRIAL RESEARCH,19, University Road, P B No. 2122, New Delhi - 110007 | http://www.shriaminstitute.org/technology-business-incubator.html | 1) Dr. Bhupesh Sharma, Manager, Shriram Institute 2) Dr. Ajay K. Tyagi, Asst. Director 1) sritbi@shriaminstitute.org 2)aktyagi@shriaminstitute.org T: 91-11-27667267, 27667860, 27667983 Fax: 91-11-27667676, 91-11-27667207 M: 9871438033 |

13	Atma Ram Sanatan Dharma College University of Delhi	1) Nanomaterials and Composite Technologies	Delhi	Delhi	zTM-Business Planning and Development (ZTM&BPD) Unit, IARI, New Delhi – 110012	http://arsdstar.wixsite.com/ciel	http//arsdstar.wixsite.com/ci el/downloads	Dr. Rajeev Singh, Incubator Manager 1) principal.arsdcollege@gmail.com 2) rajeev@arsd.du.ac.in M: 9311225501
		2) Renewable energy applications						
		3) electronics and ICT related						
		4) energy / technologies						
		5) Waste to energy technology						
		6) e-waste						
		7) mobile computing						
		8) Embedded systems						
		9) Digital image processing						
		10) Web technology						
		11) Power System and Power Electronics						

| 14 | Electropreneur Park by STPI Delhi/Delhi University/IESA | Electronics
12) foods and dairy products
13) bioinformatics
14) cheminformatics
15) research and technology development
16) material sciences | Delhi | Delhi | Electropreneur Park

3rd Floor Library Building University of Delhi South Campus
Benito Juarez Road, New Delhi -110 021 | http//electropreneurpark.res.in/ | Mr. Himanshu Shekhar, Manager Admin
himanshu@electropreneurpark.co m
M: 91-8860940000
T: 011-65164488 |

No	Name	Sectors	State	City	Address	Website	Website	Contact
15	M/s Zonal Technology Management -Business Planning and Development Unit" -ZTM-BPD, IARI, New Delhi	Agriculture & allied sectors	Delhi	Delhi	ZTM-Business Planning and Development (ZTM&BPD) Unit, IARI, New Delhi – 110012	http://ztmbpd.iari.res.in/?q=content/arise		Dr. Neeru Bhooshan, Incharge 1) zonaltech@ iari.res.in 2) ps.ztmiari@gmail.com T: +91-11-25843542, +91-11-25843553
16	Centre for Incubation and Business Acceleration	1. ICT 2. Food Processing 3. Clean Technologies	Goa	Assago	Centre for Incubation and Business Acceleration Campus of Agnel Institute of Technology and Design Agnel Technical Education Complex, Assago, Goa-403507, Goa	http://www.ciba.org.in	http://www.ciba.org.in/ services.php#incubation	D.S. Prashant, General Manager prashant@ciba. org.in M: 9823235890
17	CIIIE Initiatives, Centre for Innovation, Incubation and Entrepreneurship (CIIE)	Market oriented products/ technologies (ICT, Renewable energy, Social impact)	Gujarat	Ahmedabad	CIIE, IIM new campus, Sargam Marg, Vastrapur, Ahmedabad, Gujarat 3800015	http://www.ciie.co/	http://www.ciie.co/start-up/	Mr. Neeraj Jain, Manager neeraj@iima.ac.in T: 079-6632 4203 Fax: 079-66324207

No.	Name	Sector	State	City	Address	URL	Contact URL	Contact Person
18	Gujarat Foundation for Entrepreneurial excellence-icreate	Technology & innovation	Gujarat	Ahmedabad	International Centre for Entrepreneurship and Technology — First floor, GMDC Building, 132 Ft Ring Road, Vastrapur, Ahmedabad 380 052, India	http://icreate.org.in/	http://icreate.org.in/contact	Mr. Anupam Lavania, Manager; anupam@icreate.org.in; M: 079-27912803
19	IITGN Incubation Centre	Technology	Gujarat	Gandhinagar	IIT Gandhinagar near village palaj, gandhinagar-382355	https://www.iitgn.ac.in/sites/ default/files/IIEC-Brochure-2016.pdf		Mr. Anand Pandey; anandp@iitgn.ac.in; M: 07069021616
20	Comcubator (www.micaedc.org)	Communication technology	Gujarat	Ahmedabad	Shela, Ahmedabad -380 058,; Gujarat, India	https://www.mica.ac.in/edc/; mica-incubator	https://www.mica.ac.in/edc/mica-incubator	Prof U T Rao, Chairperson; rao@micamail.in; T: 02717 308319; Fax: 02717 308249; M: 9979777284

No.	Name	Category	State	City	Address	Website	Contacts
21	Gujarat State Biotechnology Mission (GSBTM), Savli Bio Incubator	Biotechnology	Gujarat	Vadodara	Block 11, 9th floor, GH Rd, Sector 11, Gandhinagar, Gujarat-382010	http://www.savlibioincubator.in/	1) Shri. S.N.Tyagi, Mission Director & Project Director 2) Dr. A. N. Bhadalkar,Sector Specialist & Project co-coordinator 3) Mrs. Anaqua Bhadalkar, Sector Specialist & Project co-coordinator 1) mdbtm@gujarat.gov.in 2) ssibtm@gujarat.gov.in 3) gujaratbiotech@gmail.com 4) info@savlibioincubator.In T: 079-23252197, 079-232 52164, 2667266000

No	Name	Sector	State	City	Address	Website	Application Link	Contact
22	B. V. Patel Pharmaceutical Education & Research Development (PERD) Centre	Biotechnology	Gujarat	Ahmedabad	Thaltej-Gandhinagar Highway, Thaltej, Ahmedabad-380054	http://perdcentre.com/BIRAC.html		Dr. Neeta Shrivastava, Assistant Director 1) perd@perdcentre.com 2) neetas@perdcentre.com T: 079 27439375/27441640
23	Ahmedabad University Support Foundation, Venture Studio, Ahmedabad University	1) Healthcare 2) Education 3) Energy 4) Transport 5) Agritech 6) Hardware & Manufacturing	Gujarat	Ahmedabad	Venture Studio, A G TeatDher's Caōpus, Commerce Six Roads, Navrangpura, Ahmedabad -380009	http://www.venturestudio.in/	https//bit.ly/vs-apply	Ms. Shanti Menon, Management Administration vs@ ahduni.edu.in T: 07926646 3150

#	Institution	Focus areas	State	City	Address	Website	Link	Contact
24	Innovation & Incubation Centre (IIC) Pandit Deendayal Petroleum University (PDPU)	1) Energy and Aligned areas 2) IT 3) E commerce	Gujarat	Gandhinagar	Innovation and incubation centre, 7 Ameinty Centre, Near Medical Centre, PDPU Campus Raisan Village, Dist Gandhinagar-382007	http://www.iic.pdpu.ac.in/voca.html	http://iic.pdpu.ac.in/istart.html	Shani Panyda, Executive shani.pandya@iic.pdpu.ac.in T: 9409611194 / 07923275163
25	Society for Innovation & Entrepreurship in Dairying (SINED) Technology Business Incubator	Dairy technology	Haryana	Karnal	Business Planning & Development (BPD) Unit, Dairy Technology Division, National Dairy Research Institute, Karnal-132001	http://www.ndritbi.com/	http://www.ndritbi.com/index.php?option=com_content&view=article&id=89&Itemid=198	Dr. Ashish Kumar Singh, Principal Scientist & Secretary, SINED-TBI aksndri@gmail.com T: 0184-2259304, 2259329
26	91springboard, Gurgaon	1) Sector neutral (vertical) 2) Internet & Mobile Technology (Horizontal)	Haryana	Gurgaon	91springboard, Plot 23, Sector 18, Maruti Industrial Area	www.91springboard.com		Pranay Gupta, Cofounder info@91springboard.com +91-9015419191

No.	Name	Sectors/Domains	State	City	Address	Website	Form Link	Contact
27	Shri Mata Vaishno Devi University Technology Business Incubation Center Society (SMVDU TBI)	1) Biotechnology (Microbial, Plant, Medical Genetics and Diagnostics) 2) Engineering (Electronics, Robotics, E-commerce, GSM/GPRS based Technology, Alternative Energy Management) 3) Business Development	Jammu & Kashmir	Katra	Academic Blocks, B-C Junction, 2nd Floor Shri Mata Vaishno Devi University Campus, Katra Jammu and Kashmir, India -182320.	http://smvdutbic.org/tbic/	http://goo.gl/forms/tlk92yajZw	Dr Swarkar Sharma, Interim CEO smvdu.tbic@smvdu.ac.in T: 01991-285535 // 285524 // 285634 // 285699 extn: 2385
28	Indo Danish Tool Room	Mechanical	Jharkhand	Jamshedpur	M-4,(Part),Phase-VI, Tata Kansdra Road,P.O. Gamharia, Jamshedpur-832108			Mr.Ashutosh Kumar, Dy. General Manager reach@idtrjamshedpur.com T: 0657-2201261/62 Fax: 0657-2202723

#	Name	Sectors	State	City	Address	Website	Contact
29	NASSCOM-ERNET Center Of Excellence (CoE) For Internet Of Things (IoT)	Agriculture, Healthcare, Energy, Transportation, Emerging Technologies	Karnataka	Bangalore	#150 Diamond District, HAL Airport Road, Bangalore 560008		Sanjeev Malhotra, CEO Coe-iot@nasscom.in 080 41693924
30	Composites Technology Park (www.compositestechnologypark.com)	Composites based on coir, bamboo, jute	Karnataka	Bangalore	205, Bande Mutt, Kengeri Satellite Township, Bangalore -560060	www.composites technologypark.com	Dr. R Gopalan, Executive Director drgopalan2003@yahoo.com T: 6б6-cqejc6q / cqθθ6θ6q / 28482768 Fax: 080-28482771
31	Syndicate	1) Blockchain 2) Internet of things 3)Fintech 4)Logistic Technology	Karnataka	Bangalore	81/37, 2nd Floor; The Hulkul Lavelle Road; Bengaluru 560001	http://www.thesyndicate. tech /	Rammohan, rammohan. prabhakar@thesyndicat e.tech M:9845288752

32	IIITB Innovation Center	IT	Karnataka	Bangalore	IIIT-Bangalore 26/C, Electronics City, Hosur Road, Bangalore -560100.	http://www.iiitb.org/	Mr. D.V.Jagadish, CEO 1) startup@iiitb.org 2) dv.jagadish@iiitb.ac.in T: +91 80 4140 7777 Fax: +91 80 4140 7704
33	MSME Business Incubator.	1) IT	Karnataka	Nitte	Nitte-574110, Karkalla Taluk	http://nmamit.nitte.edu.in/	Dr. Balasubramani R., Chief Project Leader – EDC 1)balasubramni.r@ nitte.edu.in 2)info@nitte.edu.in Fax: 91-0824-2204305,08258-281265 M: 9900462705
		2) Biotech					
34	Science & Technology Entrepreneurs Park (BECSTEP)	1) Food Processing	Karnataka	Bagalkot	STEP Road,Behind BTDA Capmus, Bagalkot-587102	http://www.becbgk.edu/step.php	Dr Bharti S. Executive Director M:9448972628
		2) Textiles					
		3) Building Technology					

No.	Name	Sectors/Focus Areas	State	City	Address	Website	Contact
35	STEP-SJCE	1) Electronics & IT 2) Automotive design 3) Mobile applications 4) Data analytics 5) Embedded systems 6) Energy conservation 7) E-marketing	Karnataka	Mysore	Manasagangothri, Mysore-570006	http://www.sjcestep.in/	Dr. B G Sangamashwera, Chief Executive info@sjcestep.in T: 0821-2548321 Fax: 0821-2548321
36	Global Incubation Services (GINSERVE) (Web: www.ginserve.in)	Technology	Karnataka	Bangalore	Global Incubation Services CA Site No:1 HAL 3rd Stage, Behind Hotel Leela Palace, Kodihalli, Bangalore -560008, Karnataka, India.	http://www.ginserv.in/	Mr. Vinod Shankar, COO vinod@ginserv.in M: 984575103
37	Nadathur S Raghavan Centre for Entrepreneurial Learning (NSRCEL)	Agnostic	Karnataka	Bangalore	NRSCEL, Indian institute of Management Bangalore, Bannerghatta Road, Sundar Ram, Shetty Nagar, Bilekahalli, Bengaluru 5600076	http://www.nsrcel.org/ http://www.nsrcel.org/register/	Rajiv Sawhney, COO rajiv.sawhney@IIMB.ERNET.IN M: +91-8026993758

38	C-CAMP Bioincubator	1) Life Sciences 2) Biotechnology	Karnataka	Bangalore	Centre for Cellular and Molecular Platforms NCBS-TIFR Campus, GKVK Post, Bellary Road, Bangalore 560065, India	www.ccamp.res.in		Dr. Taslimarif Saiyed, Director and COO (C-CAMP) taslim@ccamp.res.in T: 91-80-6718-5100
39	National Design Business Incubator (NDBI)	Design	Karnataka	Bengaluru	B-112, Rajajinagar, Industrial Estate Bengaluru-560044	www.ndbiindia.org		Srinath Bhadram, Manager manager. ndbi.b@nid.edu M: 9902067555 T: 080-23408200
40	Technovate Innovations	1) Healthcare 2) Logistics	Karnataka	Bangalore	L-142 5th Avenue 5th Main HSR Layout Sec 6 Bangalore -560 102. P: +91 804-653-4800	http://venturefactory.in	http://venturefactory.in/get-startup-funded/	Mr. Vincent Rajendran, Director Operations v.rajendran@i2india.in M: 9535724747

No.	Company	Sector	State	City	Address	Website	Contact
41	LetsVenture (Indiepitch Solutions Pvt. Ltd.)	1) Technology 2) IT/ITES 3) Software 4) Hardware 5) Sector Agnostic	Karnataka	Bangalore	2nd Floor, No.7, Raja Ram Mohan Roy Road, Opposite to Ramanashree Hotel, Bengaluru, Karnataka -560025	www.letsventure.com	Atit Danak, Director atit.danak@letsventure.com -9910491224
42	Excubator Consulting Private Limited	1) IoT 2) Artificial Intelligence 3) IT +C110	Karnataka	Bangalore	Building # 758, 3rd floor,19th Main Rd, HSR Layout -Sector 2, Bengaluru, Karnataka 560102	www.excubator.org	Rakesh Mishra, Director & cofounder rakesh.mishra@excubator.org 9845032742
43	TLabs-Times Internet Limited	1) Technology 2) E-Commerce 3) Online Media 4) EdTech 5) Healthcare 6) Artificial Intelligence 7) Machine Learning 8) Internet of Things 9) AdTech 10) FinTech	Karnataka	Bangalore	TLabs, 6th Floor, Slalarpuria Tower, Biz Bazaar Building, Next to Forum Mall, Koramangla, Bangalore	http://tlabs.in/	Abhishek Mitra Gupta, Chief Operating Officer adhishek@tlads.in +∈6-∈θ6αxθxϕθj

No.	Name	Technology	State	City	Address	Website	Application Link	Contact
44	Amal-Jyothi Rural Technologies Business Incubator	1) Rural Technology 2) Green Technology 3) Information Technology	Kerala	Kanjirappally	Koovappally, Kanjirappally, Kottayam (Dist),Kerala -686518	http://www.ajce.in/tbihome	http://www.ajce.in/tbihome/tbiapplication/	Mr. Jose Kannampuzha, Principal principal@ amaljyothi. ac.in T: + 91 4828 305503, 305626 M: 9496805712
45	Startup Village	Agnostic	Kerala	Kochi	1st Floor, atop Café Coffee day, 4th Block, 80 Feet Main Road, Kormangala, Bangalore-560095	https://www.sv.co/	https://sv.co/apply	Mr. Sanjay Vijayakumar, Chairmain and Managing Director sanjay@sv.co M: 9846819123
46	CET -Technology Business Incubator	1) Green Technology 2) IT	Kerala	Trivandrum	College of Engineering, Trivandrum, Kerala - 695016	http://www.cet.ac.in/	http://cet-edccet.rhcloud.com/about.html	Dr. A Samson, Coordinator asamson64@ gmail.com T: 0471-2515502, 0471-2515556 M: 9447324844
47	KSIDC, Thiruvananthapuram	Biotech	Kerala	Thiruvananthapuram	KSIDC Ltd., Kowdiar Post, Trivandrum	http://www.ksidc.org/		Biju B G, Assistant General Manager bijubg@ ksidcmail.org M: 09847936409 T: 0471-2318922

#	Name	Categories	State	City	Address	Website	Apply/Contact Link	Contact
48	NASSCOM 10000 Startup Warehouse Kochi	1) IT Products 2) IOT 3) SAAS	Kerala	Kakkanad	NASSCOM 10000 Startup Warehouse, Infopark Campus, Kakkanad, Kerala 682030	http://10000startups.com/startup-warehouse/		Arun Nair, Deputy Manager arun@nasscom.in T: 0484 2415140/50
49	TBI (http://nitc.ac.in/misc/tbi/public_html/index.htm)	1) IT & electronics 2) Agriculture Engineering 3) Nano-tech	Kerala	Calicut	NITC, Calicut -673601	http://www.tbi.nitc.ac.in/	http://www.tbi.nitc.ac.in/howtoapply.php	Dr. Abraham T Mathew, Chairman, TBI (Dean -Research & Consultancy) NITC atm@nitc.ac.in T: 0495-2286144 M: 9447087949 FAX: 0495-2287250
50	Technopark TBI	1) IT 2) Electronics 3) Biotechnology 4) E-learning 5) Bio informatics 6) Social Entrepreneurship	Kerala	Thiruvananthapuram	Technopark TBI Technopark Campus Trivandrum -695 581	http://www.technopark.org/	http://www.technopark.org/contact-us	Dr. Jayasankar Prasad, CEO T-TBI ceo@startupmission.in T: 471-2700270 Fax: 471-2700171

	Name	Sector	State	City	Address	Website	Website	Contact
51	Amrita TBI	IT	Kerala	Kollam	Amritapuri Campus, Clappana, P.O Kollam, Kerala -690525	http://amritatbi.com/	http://amritatbi.com/incubation.htm	Snehal Shetty, Vice President snehal@amritatbi.com T: 0476 280 5454
52	Technology Business Incubator for Medical Devices	1) Medical devices	Kerala	Trivandrum	5th Floor, MS Valiathan Building, Biomedical Technology Wing, Sree Chitra Triunal Institute for Medical Science & Technology, Poojapura, Trivandrum, Kerala	http://tiimed.org.in/	http://tiimed.org.in/contacts.html	Dr. S. BALRAM, CEO tiimed@sctimst.ac.in M: 9249402311
	& Biomaterials (SCTIMST-TIMed)	2) Biomaterials						
		3) Healthcare						
53	KSIDC Business Incubation Centre (KSIDC-BIC)	IT & ITES	Kerala	Kochi	KSIDC BIC, Geo Infopark,KINFRA Park, Kakkanad, Kochi	http://www.ksidc.org		Shri. R.Prasanth-Deputy General Manager: prasanth@ksidcmail.org + 91-9847340444
54	Technology Innovation and Incubation Centre (TIIC)	ITES & Products	Madhya Pradesh	Gwalior	E-007, Ground Floor, ABV-IIITM, Gwalior Morena Link Road,Gwalior, Madhya Pradesh-474015	http://www.tiiciiitm.com/	http://www.tiiciiitm.com/for m.pdf	Dr.Anurag Srivastava, Coordinator profanurag@gmail.com T:(O) 0751-2449826 M: +91-9826189049

No.	Name	Type	State	City	Address	Website	Contact
55	Venture Center	Agnostic	Maharashtra	Pune	Venture Center, National Chemical Laboratory 100 NCL Innovation Park National Chemical Laboratory Campus Pune -411008	http://www.venturecenter. co.	Dr. V. Premnath, Director 1) v.premnath@ncl.res.in 2) director@venturecenter. co.in ,020-2590-2185 Fax: 91-20-2589-3104 Phone: 020-2590-2986, 020-6401-1024
61	NASSCOM 10000 Start Ups Warehouse – Navi Mumbai	1) IT and enabled Technologies	Maharashtra	Mumbai	Unit no. 304, Bldg 2, Sector 1, Millennium Business Park, Navi Mumbai, Maharashtra 400710	http://10000startups. com/10k-program/ http://10000startups.com/ sta rtup-warehouse-form/	Sahil Gupta, Deputy Manager sahil@nasscom.in T: 022-27784414
62	UnLtd India	Social Startups	Maharashtra	Mumbai	Block no 1, Flat No 1&2, Baitul Karim building, 4 Boran Road, Bandra (W), Mumbai 400 050	http://www.unltdindia. org/ http://www.unltdindia. org/incubation/apply/	

63	MITCON Technology Business Incubation Centre (A Division of MITCON)	1) Biotechnology	Maharashtra	Pune	Near DIC, Agriculture College Campus, Shivajinagar, Pune - 411005	https://www. mitconbiopharma.com	http://www. mitconbiopharma	Dr. Pradeep Bavadekar, Managing Director md@mitconindia.com T: 020 -66289452
	Consultancy & Engg. Services Ltd.)	2) Ayurveda					.com/wp-content/ uploads/2015/12/ Incubatee-Application-Format.pdf	M: 08308809265
		3) Biomedicine						
		4) Renewable Energy						
		5) Environment						
		6) IT						
		7) Engineering electronic sectors						

64	Science And Technology Park	1) Open Source & Open Platform Technology 2) Renewable Energy & Clean Technology 3) Pharma & Biotechnology 4) Mobile Computing 5) Project Management 6) Data Centers 7) Social Incubation 8) IT/ITES 9) Education 10) Agri & Food Processing Technology 11) Remote Sensing & GIS 12) Electronics & Telecommunications 13) Cyber Security 14) Health	Maharashtra	Pune	Savitribai Phule Pune University Campus, Ganeshkhind Road, Pune -411007	http://scitechpark.org.in/	Dr.Rajendra P.Jagdale, Director General stp@scitechpark.org.in T: +91-20-25699206 / 25693449

65	SINE (Society for Innovation & Entrepreneurship)	Agnostic	Maharashtra	Mumbai	3rd Floor CSRE Building, IIT Bombay Campus, Powai -400 076	http://sineiitb.org/sine/home /	http://sineiitb.org/sine/incub ation/apply/	Mr. Rakesh Rajiv, Business Executive 1) sine@sineiitb.org 2) rakesh@sineiitb.org T: +91 22 2576 7016 Fax: +91 22 2572 1220
66	DKTE Technology Business Incubator	Clothing and textile technology	Maharashtra	Kolhapur	D.K.T.E.Society's Textile & Engineering Institute, P.O.Box-130 Rajlada, Ichalkaranji-416 115. Dist-Kolhapur. Maharashtra.	http://www.dktetbi.com/	http://www.dktetbi.com/tbi_Incubation.htm	Prof.(Dr.) P.V.Kadole, Principal pvkadole@gmail.com T: 0230-2421300
67	NASSCOM 10000 Startup Warehouse Pune	1) IT 2) Software	Maharashtra	Pune	NASSCOM 10000 Startup Warehouse,4th Floor,406,MIDC IT tower,Kharadi,Pune 411014	www.10000startups.com		Darryl Zuzarte, Manager darryl@nasscom.in M: 9850813443

	Incubator	Sectors	State	City	Address	Website	Contact
68	Trident Business Incubator	1) Biotech	Odisha	Bhubaneswar	Plot no: F2/A,Chandaka		Mr. Santosh Kumar Sahoo, Assistant Professor 1) edcell@tat.ac.in
		2) Internet Startup			Industrial Estate,Infocity Area, Chandrasekharpur, Bhubaneswar-751024		2) esantoshsahoo@gmail. Com
		3) Engineering Industry					M: 9861387561
69	KIIT -Technology Business Incubator (KIITTBI)	1) Functional food	Odisha	Bhubaneswar	KIIT Technology Business Incubator KIIT School of Biotechnology, Campus -11	http://www.kiitincubator. in/	http://www.kiitincubator. in/pdf/tbiapplicationform. pdf
		2) Bioinformatics					Dr. Mrutyunjay Suar, CEO
		3) Exploitive Micro-biology			KIIT University Patia, Bhubaneswar,		mrutyunjay@ kiitincubator.in
		4) Agri-tech & Information Technology					M: 9437011465
		5) Electronics and engineering products			Orissa, INDIA		
70	Guru Nanak Dev Engineering College STEP	1) Mechanical	Punjab	Ludhiana	SCIENCE AND	http://stepgndec.com/	Prof. Nirmal Singh, Executive Director contact@stepgndec.in step. gne@gmail.com
		2) IT			TECHNOLOGY		T: 0161-2814748 M:9855020485
					ENTREPRENEURS' PARK		
					Near Guru Nanak Dev Engineering College, Gill, Ludhiana – 6x666c India		

#	Name	Sectors	State	City	Address	Website	Application Link	Contact
71	Science and Technology Entrepreneur's Park (STEP)	1) Biotechnology 2) IT 3) Electronics 4) Mechanical	Punjab	Patiala	Thapar University, Patiala	http://www.thapar.edu		Dr. Dinesh Goyal, Executive Director dgoyal@thapar.edu M: +91 9815601705
72	Startup Oasis	Agnostic	Rajasthan	Jaipur	RIICO Software Complex, EPIP, Sitapura Industrial Area, Jaipur-302022, Rajasthan (India)	http://startupoasis.in/	http://startupoasis.in/howtoapply.php	Mr. Dilnawaz Khan, Program Manager connect@startupoasis.in M: 9887027865
73	BITS Pilani-Technology Business Incubator	Embdedded systems & VLSI designs	Rajasthan	Pilani	Bits Pilani, Vidya Vihar, Pilani, Rajasthan, PIN - 333031	http://www.bits-pilani.ac.in/pilani/technology business/TechnologyBusinessIncubator	http://www.bits-pilani.in/Uploads/MicroModule/2011-12-17–0-17-59-528_Application_Form_bitsweb.pdf	Dr. Anu Gupta, Program Manager anug@pilani.bits-ilani.ac.in T: +91-1596-51-5694, 9828125263 Fax: 91 01596 244183
74	A.C.Tech Campus	Biotech Engineering	Tamil Nadu	Chennai	Sardar Patel Road, Anna University, Chennai-60025	https://www.annauniv.edu		Dr.B.A.Muralidhar, Assistant Director – murlidharba@annauniversity.edu M: 9444539875

#	Name	Sectors	State	City	Address	Website	Contact
75	Adhiyamaan College of Engineering -TBI	1) GPS 2) ICT based system	Tamil Nadu	Hosur	Technology Business Incubator Development of Entrepreneurship Through Incubation, DETI@ACE Adhiyamaan College of Engineering Campus, Dr.M.G.R Nagar, Hosur, Krishnagiri(Dt), Tamil Nadu-635109, India	http://www.detiace.com/	S Gobinath, Technical Manager DETI@ACE tmdetiace@gmail.com T: 04344-261011, 04344-261020 M: 9092327244
76	Bannari Amman Institute of Technology- Technology Business Incubator (BIT-TBI)	Biotechnology in Agro, Industrial and Rural sectors	Tamil Nadu	Sathyamangalam	Bannari Amman Institute of Technology -Technology Business Incubator(BIT-TBI) Sathyamangalam-638401, Erode District, Tamil Nadu	http://www.bittbi.com/	Dr K BALAKRISHNAN, Principal Scientist & Head Professor balu444@gmail.com T: 04295-221298(Direct), 04295-226321
77	Centre for Entrepreneurship Development and Incubation (CEDI)	1) IT 2) Electronics	Tamil Nadu	Tiruchirappalli	National Institute of Technology, Tiruchirappalli 620015, Tamil Nadu, India.	http://www.nitt.edu/home/other/cedi/	Dr. G. Kannabiran, Project Investigator-CEDI cedi@nitt.edu T: 0431-2503003
						http://nitt-cedi.in/download-student-projects.php	

No.	Name	Sector	State	City	Address	Website	Contact
78	Healthcare Technology Innovation Centre	Medical Devices	Tamil Nadu	Chennai	Healthcare Technology Innovation Centre (HTIC), 3E, 3rd Floor, IIT Madras Research Park Kanagam Road, Taramani, Chennai – c66 sqft.	https://htic.iitm.ac.in/newsite/	Muthu Singaram, Incharge director@htic.iitm.ac.in M: 9790932420
79	Jeppiaar Engineering College	1) Mechanical 2) Biotechnology 3) Electronics and instrumentation engineering 4) Aeronautical engineering 5) Computer Science 6) IT	Tamil Nadu	Chennai	Jeppiaar Nagar, Rajiv Gandhi Salai,Chennai-600119	http://www.sathyabamauniversity.ac.in/phd/supervisorDetail.php?ref=31055	Dr.M.Sasikumar, Professor In-Charge pmsasi77@gmail.com M: 9094277053
80	Kongu Engineering College -TBI	1) Electronics 2) ICT	Tamil Nadu	Perundurai	TBI @ KEC, Kongu Engineering College Campus, Perundurai – 638 052, Erode, TamilNadu	http://www.tbi-kec.org/ http://www.tbi-kec.org/downloads.php	Mr. P.S.Kannan, Manager 1) tbi-kec@ kongu.ac.in 2) tbi_kec@yahoo.com T: 04294 226650 T: 4294 226633 M: 99439 27275

No.	Name	Sectors	State	City	Address	Website	Contact
81	Periyar Technology Business Incubator	1) Agro, bio and food technologies; 3) Manufacturing; 2) Herbal products	Tamil Nadu	Thanjavur	Business Incubator Periyar Maniammai University Periyar Nagar, Vallam Thanjavur-613 403, Tamil Nadu.	http://www.periyartbi.org/ptbi/index.php	Ms. A.P.Aruna, Chief Executive Officer info@ periyartbi.org T: 91+4362-264520, 9944495659 Fax: 91+4362-264660
82	RMK Engineering College -Incubation Center	ITeS	Tamil Nadu	Kavaraipettai	RSM Nagar, Gummidipoondi Taluk, Tiruvallur District, Kavaraipettai, Tamil Nadu 601206	http://www.rmkec.ac.in	Dr. Elwin Chandra Monie, Principal principal@rmkec.ac.in T: 044-33303331/ 33303330 M: 9443627226

83	Sathyabama University – Technology Business Incubator	1) Functional food	Tamil Nadu	Chennai	Sathyabama University -Technology Business Incubator,	http://sathyabamatbi.in/	Mr Kartik, Manager sathyabamauniversitybi@gmail.co m
		2) Bioinformatics			Jeppiaar Nagar, Rajiv Gandhi Road, Chennai – c666666.		M: 9443928573
		3) Exploirive Micro-biology					
		4) Agri-tech & Information Technology					
		5) Electronics and engineering products					
84	Tiruchirappalli Regional Engineering College - Science and Technology Entrepreneurs Park (TRECSTEP)	1) Mechanical	Tamil Nadu	Tiruchirappalli	Tiruchirappalli Regional Engineering College Science and Technology Entrepreneurs Park TREC-STEP,	http://www.trecstep.com/	R.M.P. Jawahar, Executive Director jawa_rs@yahoo. com
		2) IT					T: +91-431-2500085 & 2500697
					Tiruchirappalli-620015, India.		Fax: +91-431-2500175

85	University of Madras -TBI	1) Manufacturing	Tamil Nadu	Chennai	UOM-TBI University of Madras Dr, A L M PGIBMS, Taramani campus, Chepauk Chennai -600113	http://www. unom. ac.in/index. php?route=department/ department/ about&deptid-69	Dr. G. Gangi Reddy, Managing Director 1) tbi@ unom.ac.in 2) tbi_unom@ yahoo.com M: 9840597373
		2) Healthcare					
		3) Engineering					
		4) IT					
		5) IoT					
86	Vel TeDh – Technology Incubator	1) Waste Management	Tamil Nadu	Chennai	Vel Tech Technology Incubator	http://www.veltechtbi. com/ http://www. veltechtbi.com/pr	Mr Chandrakumar, Manager vtu@veltechuniv. edu.in T: 044 26840605 Fax: 044 26840605 M: 9600040254
		specifically for E-waste			No 42, Vel Tech Road, Avadi,		
		2) Bio waste			Chennai – c66 6ct		
		3) Plastics waste			Tamil Nadu		
		4) 3D Printing					
		5) Embedded Systems/VLSI					
		6) Micro Air Vehicles (MAV)/ Robotics					
		7) Automobile					
		8) Renewable Energy					
		9) IT/ITES.					

87	Er.Perumal Manimekalai College of Engineering	Brick Manufacturing	Tamil Nadu	Hosur	17th KM Hosur, Krishnagiri highways, Koneripalli, Hosur , 635117,TN	http://www.pmctech.org		Dr.S.Chitra schitra@gmail.com M: 9787009790
88	A.C.College of Engineering & Technology	Civil Engineering	Tamil Nadu	Karaikudi	Alagappa Chettiar College of Engineering and Technology Karaikudi-630004,TN	http://www.accet.edu.in		Dr A Sivanantharaja, Associate Professor accet.principal@gmail.com M: 9443919844
89	Agribusiness Development -Tamil Nadu Agricultural University	Agribusiness	Tamil Nadu	Coimbatore	The Directorate of Agri Business Development, Tamil Nadu Agricultural University, Coimbatore -641 003.	https://sites.goole.com/a/tnau.ac.in/dabd/home	https://sites.google.com/a/tnau.ac.in/dabd/membership	Dr R Murugesan, Director business@tnau.ac.in M: 9489056714
90	Coimbatore Innovation and Business Incubator -Kumaraguru College of Technology	1) Electronics (IoT) 2) Technology Services (Industrial/ Engineering Design, Automation)	Tamil Nadu	Coimbatore	FORGE.FACTORY G Floor, KCT Tech Park, #3 Athipalayam Road, Chinnavedapatri, Coimbatore 641049.	http://www.forgeforward.in/	https://goo.gl/forms/JthDVzb7UHCQBxyJ2	Mr. Vishwanathan Sahasranamam, Vice President info@forgeforward.in T: +917598446822

No.	Name	Sectors	State	City	Address	Website	Contacts
91	Dr A.P.J. Abdul Kalam Business Incubator -Vinayaka Mission's Kirupanana Variyar engineering college	1) Biotech 2) Food Processing 3) Electronics equipment design 4) Mechanical equipment design	Tamil Nadu	Salem	Sanskari Road(NH-47), Periya seeragapadi, Salem -636308,Tamil Nadu	http://www.vmkvec.ac.in/	Dr. A.Nagappan, Principal principal.vmkvec@vmu.edu.in M: 9842957514, 9362121432
92	K.L.N.College of Engineering	IT	Tamil Nadu	Madurai	Nedukulam road, Pottapalayam post, Sivagangai district, Madhurai-630612	http://www.klnce.edu	1) Dr. A.V. Ramprasad,Head of Institution 2) Dr Pradeep Kanan, Manager Incubation centre principal@klnce.edu 1) M: 9940125238 2) M: 9894770741

93	Nanotech Research Innovation and Incubation Centre (NRIIC) -PSG	Nanotechnology	Tamil Nadu	Coimbatore	Nanoresearch Facility (PSG Institute of Advanced Studies	http://www.psgias.ac.in/?page_id=5150	1) Prof. KK Venkataraman, Prof in charge
	Institute of Advanced Studies				Coimbatore-641004)		2) Dr. K.Suresh Kumar, Manager
							1) kkv@psgias. ac.in
							2) step@psgtech.edu
							1) T: +91-422-4344000 extn 4323
							M: 9500950311
							Fax: +91-422-2573833
							2) T: +91-422-363300, 4363301
							Fax: +91-422-2573833

#	Name		State	City	Address	Website	Contact
94	PSG-STEP	1) Mechanical	Tamil Nadu	Coimbatore	PSG-Science & Technology Entrepreneurial Park (PSG-STEP) C-Block, Ground Floor PSG College of Technology Coimbatore -641 004 Tamil Nadu. INDIA	http://www.psgias.ac.in/?page_id=5150 http://www.psgstep.org/	1) Prof. KK Venkataraman, Prof in charge; 2) Dr. K.Suresh Kumar, Manager step@psgtech.edu kv@psgias.ac.in T: +91-422-4363300, 4363301 Fax: +91-2573833
		2) IT					
		3) Nano Technology					
		4) Electronics					
95	Sri Ramakrishna Engineering College	ICT	Tamil Nadu	Coimbatore	Vattamalaipalayam, N.G.G.O. Colony Post, Coimbatore-641022	http://www.srec.ac.in	Dr Metilda, Cordinator metilda@srec.ac.in M: 9442952055
96	St. Peter's Engineering College -TBI	1) Refrigeration	Tamil Nadu	Chennai	Technology business Incubator St.Peter's Engineering College Avadi, Chennai Tamil Nadu, India.	http://www.spectbi.com/ http://www.spectbi.com/selection_process.html	Dr. L. Mahesh Kumar, CEO info@spectbi.com M: +91-9840024189
		2) Cold chain					
		3) IT					
		4) Mechanical					

No.	Name	Sector	State	City	Address	Website	Apply Link	Contact
97	Technology Business Incubator Centre for Biotechnology -Anna University	Biotechnology	Tamil Nadu	Chennai	Technology Business Incubator Centre for Biotechnology, Anna University, Chennai - 600025	https://www.annauniv.edu/ct dt/contents/technology/biote ch.html		Dr. S.Meenakshisundaram, Business Manager; meenakshi@annauniv.edu; T: 044-22358363; 2,23,50,77,22,23,58,360; M: 98403 48173; Fax 044 22350299
98	VIT Technology Business Incubator	1) Bio-Technology based industries 2) Environmental friendly solutions and products for Leather industries 3) Automotive / Mechanical Engineering sector related	Tamil Nadu	Vellore	VIT -Technology Business Incubator, Vellore Institute of Technology, Vellore, Tamil Nadu India.	http://www.vittbi.com/#	http://vittbi.com/#/apply	Mr A. Balachandran, General Manager vittbi@vit.ac.in T: +91 416 224 3097

		products and services						
		4) Information Technology Products and Solutions						
99	National Engineering College-Business Incubator	1) Manufacturing 2) Energy	Tamil Nadu	Kovilpatti	National Engineering College, K.R.Nagar,Kovilpatti, Thoothukudi district-628503,TN	http://www.nec.edu.in	http://www.nec.edu.in/ necbi	Dr.S.Shanmugavel, Principal principal@ nec.edu.in T: 04632-222502, 230227
		3) Electronics and Trading 4) Agriculture						
100	IITM's Rural Technology Business Incubator	1) Rural/ Underserved societal segments 2) ICT (Information and Communication Technologies)	Tamil Nadu	Chennai	Module 6, 1st Floor, IITM Research Park, Kangam Road, Taramani, Chennai -600113	http://www.rtbi.in/	http://www.rtbi.in/ Incubation%20MIS/ incubation_application. php	Dr. Tamaswati Ghosh, CEO tamaswati@incubation. iitm.ac.in T:+91 44 66469872
102	IIT Madras-Incubation Cell	Agnostic	Tamil Nadu	Chennai	IITM Incubation Cell	http://www.incubation. iitm.a c.in/home	http://www.incubation. iitm.ac.in/incubation/ apply	Dr. Tamaswati Ghosh, CEO 1)office@incubation. iitm.ac.in 2) tamaswati@ incubation. iitm.ac.in
					A2 03, Third Floor, IIT Madras Research Park Kanagam Road, Taramani Chennai -600113, Tamil Nadu, India			T: +91 44 66469869

No.	Name	Sectors	State	City	Address	Website	Website 2	Contact
103	Villgro Innovations Foundation	1) Agriculture 2) Education 3) Energy Health	Tamil Nadu	Chennai	3rd Floor, IIT Madras Research park, Kanagam Road, Taramani (Behind Tidel Park, on old Mahabalipuram Road), Chennai -600113	http://www.villgro.org	http://www.villgro.org/incubation-apply	Ms Chaarvi Badani, EA to President info@villgro.org T: 044 66630400
104	IIT Madras Research Park	Agnostic	Tamil Nadu	Chennai	IIT Madras Research Park, Kanagam Road, Taramani, Chennai -600 113.	http://respark.iitm.ac.in/		Dr. Tamaswati Ghosh, CEO tamaswati@incubation.iitm.ac.in T: +91 44 66469872
105	Association for Innovation Development of Entrepreneurs in Agriculture (A-IDEA) -NAARM	Agriculture	Telangana	Hyderabad	ICAR-National Academy of Agricultural Research Management, Rajendra Nagar, Hyderabad-500 030	http://www.aidea.naarm.org.in	http://www.naarm.ernet.in/index.php?option=com_content&view=article&id=117:a-idea&catid=28&Itemid=4358&lang=en#contact	Mr Vijay Nadimti, COO naarmtbi.aidea@gmail.com T: +91 40 24581427 M: +91 99899 28773 Fax: +91-40 24015912
106	Centre for Technology Business Incubator (BITS Pilani)	1) Embedded systems 2) VLSI designs	Telangana	Hyderabad	BITS-Pilani, Hyderabad Campus, Jawahar Nagar, Shamirpet Mandal, R R Dist., Hyderabad -560078	http://www.bits-pilani.ac.in/pilani/technology business/TechnologyBusinessIncubator	http://www.bits-pilani.ac.in/Uploads/MicroModule/2011-12-17--0-17-59-528_Application_Form_bitsw eb.pdf	Dr. Anu Gupta, Program Manager anug@pilani.bits-pilani.ac.in T: +91-1596-51-5694, 9828125263 Fax: 91 01596 244183

#	Name	Domain	State	City	Address	URL 1	URL 2	Contact
7	International Institute of Information Hyderabad (IIIT)-Foundation	1) Computer vision 2) Natural languages 3) Speech recognition 4) ARNR & gaming domain	Telangana	Hyderabad	Vindhya C4, IIIT-H Campus, Gachibowli, Hyderabad, Telangana	http://iiith.org/index.html	http://iiith.org/program.html#pricing	Mr. Tom Thomas, COO 1) http://iiith.org/contact.html 2) tom@iiith.org T: 040 6653 1211
108	T-HUB	Agnostic	Telangana	Hyderabad	International Institute of Information Technology, Hyderabad(IIIT) Campus, Gachibowli, Hyderabad, Telangana-500032	http://www.t-hub.co/		Mr. Jay Krishnan, jay.krishnan@t-hub.co M:9945163858
109	NASSCOM 10K Warehouse Telangana	T and enabled Technologies	Telangana	Hyderabad	International Institute of Information Technology, Hyderabad campus, Gachibowli, Hyderabad, Telanga -500032	http://10000startups.com/10k-program/	http://10000startups.com/startup-warehouse-form/	Vijay Kumar Bawra, Manager vijay@nasscom.in M: 9831524485

No.	Sector/Area	State	City	Address	Website	Contact
110	Technology Business Incubator (University of Hyderabad) 1) Pharma 2) Biotechnology 3) Renewable energy	Telangana	Hyderabad	University of Hyderabad Prof. C.R Rao Road P.O. Central University Hyderabad -500 046, Telangana State, India	http://www.uohyd.ac.in/index.php/about-uoh?layout=edit&id=819	Dr. B.S. Rama Krishna, Administrative Co-ordinator 1)admintbi@ uohyd.ernet.in 2) dr.ramakrishna@gmail.com T: 040-23137551 M: 09885040914 Fax. 040-23011091
111	ALEAP-India Eco Friendly products	Telangana	Hyderabad	ALEAP Industrial estate, near pragathi nagar, OPP JNTU,kukatpally .	http://www.aleap.org	Mr A.Ajay Babu- Manager -projects Mrs. Lakshmi-Manager,ALEAP Incubators aleap93@gmail.com 8978988005
112	Dayalbagh Educational Institute 1) Textile 2) Apparel 3) Solar 4) Dairy 5)Electrical Vehicles	Uttar Pradesh	Agra	Dayalbagh, Agra-282005	http://www.dei.ac.in/dei/	Prof.Prem Kumar Kalra, Director 1)drpremkalra@ gmail.com 2)director@edei.ac.in M:9458553555 T: 0562-6548399/2801545 Fax: 0562-2801226

No.	Name	State	City	Address	Sectors	Website	Contact
113	Doon College of Engineering & Technology	Uttar Pradesh	Saharanpur	Sunderpur, Tehsil-Behat, Distt Saharanpur-247662, UP	1) Technology 2) Pharma 3) Agriculture	http//www.dooncolleg.in fo	Praveen Chaudhary, Additional Manager info@dooncollege.in M: 9412007104
114	IIITA Info Communication Incubation Centre (IIIC)	Uttar Pradesh	Allahabad	Indian Institute of Information Technology, Allahabad, Devghat, Jhalwa, Allahabad, Uttar Pradesh 211012	1) IT 2) Biomedical engineering		Prof. Sudip Sanyal, Professor ssanyal@iiita.ac.in M: +91-9415235180
115	IIMT College of Pharmacy	Uttar Pradesh	Greater Noida	Plot #-A-20, Knowledge park-3, greater Noida -201308	1) Pharma Industries 2) Healthcare	http//www.iimtindia.net	Dr. Mallikarjun BP, Principal iimtgnoida@ iimtindia.net Fax: 0120-2323860 M: 9990888627 T: 0120-2475025
116	Noida Institute of Engineering Technology Technology Business Incubator	Uttar Pradesh	Greater Noida	19, Knowledge Park-II, Institutional Area, Greater Noida, Gautam Budh Nagar- -201306	1) ICT 2) Biotechnology	http//niet.co.in/	Mr. S.R.Mustafa, General Manager srmustafa@niet. co.in M: 7838204509

No.	Name	Sector	State	City	Address	Website	Application URL	Contact
117	Amity Innovation Incubator		Uttar Pradesh	Noida	Amity Innovation Incubator E-3, 1st Floor, Amity University, Sector –125, Noida 201 301	http://www.amity.edu/aii	http://www.amity.edu/aii/joinamitycircle.asp	Tel No. 0120-4659000, 4392243
118	Process Cum Product Development center	1) Sporting goods 2) Handicraft 3) Leather	Uttar Pradesh	Meerut	Sports Goods Complex, Delhi Road, Meerut-250002, UP	http://www.ppdcmeerut.com		1) Mr.Sunil Gupta, Principal Director 2) VK Singh, Person in Charge info@ppdcmeerut.com M: 9410269600 (VK Singh) T: 0121-2511779
119	SIDBI Innovation and Incubation Centre	1) Technology 2) Engineering and other interdisciplinary areas	Uttar Pradesh	Kanpur	SIDBI Innovation & Incubation Center IIT Kanpur Sixth Ave, Kalyanpur, Kanpur, Uttar Pradesh 208016	http://www.iitk.ac.in/siic/d/	http://www.iitk.ac.in/siic/d/content/siic-application-form	1) Dr. Sameer Khandekar, Co ordinator 2) S. Sudha, Manager 3) Ravi Pandey,

	Name	Focus areas	State	City	Address	Website	Contact
							Senior Associate (Patents & Technology Transfer) 1)samkhan@iitk.ac.in 2) siic@iitk.ac.in 3) rpandey@iitk.ac.in 1) T: +91 -512 -2596646; +91 -512 -2596606 2) T: +91 -512 -2597057 3) T: +91 -512 -6596178
120	TBI-KIET (Krishna Institute of Engineering & Technology)	1) ICT 2) Mechanical 3) Electronics	Uttar Pradesh	Ghaziabad	TECHNOLOGY BUSINESS INCUBATOR -KIET KIET Group of Institutions, Ghaziabad (An ISO -9001 : 2008 Certified Institute) 13 km Stone, Ghaziabad-Meerut Road, Ghaziabad, U.P. (201206)	http//www.tbi-kiet.in/	Prof. Satyendra Kumar, General Manager tbikiet@gmail.com M: 9999017712

121	IAN Mentoring & Incubation Services	Agnostic			Ms. Archana Jahagirdar archana@tienewdelhi.org
122	TIDES Incubation Centre, IIT Roorkee (Technology Innovation and Development of Entrepreneurship Support Centre, IIT Roorkee)	1) Information & Communication Technology (ICT) 2) Bio Technology 3) Manufacturing and Engineering 4) Micro and Nano Electronics 5) Water, Sanitation and Solid Waste Management 6) Housing-Urban and Rural 7) New Materials including nano Materials 8) Building Materials / Construction Technology 9) Renewable Energy	Uttarakhand	Roorkee	TIDES Centre, Old Library Building, IIT Roorkee, Roorkee, Uttarakhand, 247667	Dr. Sanjeev Manhas, Associate Professor, Faculty In-Charge 1)smanhas333@gmail.com 2) tides@iitr.ac.in T: 01332-285147, 9760511744

Note: Row 121 additional columns: Unit No-1102,11 th floor, Tower-A, Advant IT Park Plot No-7, Sector-142, Noida Expressway, Noida -201305(U.P.) | Uttar Pradesh | Noida | http://delhi.tie.org/ian-incubator-powered-by-tie-delhi-ncr/

#	Name	Category	State	City	Address	Website	Website	Contact
123	IIM Calcutta Innovation Park	1) Social Enterprises 2) MSME	West Bengal	Kolkata	IIM CALCUTTA INNOVATION PARK IIM Calcutta, Diamond Harbour Road, P.O. Joka, Kolkata – j6o6x	http://www.iimcip.org/	http://www.iimcip.org/incubation/apply/	Mr. Subhrangshu Sanyal, CEO, subhrangshu.sanyal@iimcip.org T: +91 33 2467 8313 (Extn 576/577/541)
124	Technology Incubation and Entrepreneurship Society (TIETS)	Agnostic	West Bengal	Kharagpur	Science & Technology Entrepreneurs' Park (STEP) Indian Institute of Technology Kharagpur, India-721302.	http://www.step-iit.org/about_tiets.html	http://www.step-iit.org/about_tiets.html	1) Dr. Satyahari Dey, Professor, Managing Director 2) Prof. Siddhartha Das, Executive Adviser 3) Mr. Subhash Chandra Santra, General Manager mdstep@hijli.iitkgp.emet.in 1) T: 91-3222-283760 or-282247 (Office), -277097 (Res.), -281366 (laboratory) Fax: 91-3222-255303 or-278707. 2) T: +91-3222-283256,+91-3222-281091 3) T: 03222-281091

No.	Name	Technology	State	City	Address	Website	Application	Contact
125	Nasscom 10000 Startups Warehouse Kolkata	Technology	West Bengal	Kolkata	Nasscom Startup Warehouse, Monibhandar Building (7th. Floor), Webel Bhavan Premises,Block EP-GP, Sector-V, Salt Lake, Kolkata-700091,	http://10000startups.com	http://10000startups.com/startup-warehouse-form/	Ravi Ranjan, Manager ravi@nasscom.in M: 9874443395
126	Tagore Centre for Green Technology Business Incubation	Agnostic	West Bengal	Howrah	TAGORE CENTRE FOR GREEN TECHNOLOGY BUSINESS INCUBATION (TCGTBI) P.O. -Botanic Garden Howrah -711103 West Bengal, India	http://tcgtbi.iiests.ac.in/index	http://tcgtbi.iiests.ac.in/linkedpages/Application_Startup_Recommendation.html	Pratho Chakraborty, General Manager 1) mksanyal@rcgtbi.org 2) hodhrm@becs.ac.in T: 033-26681073 Fax: 033-26689925 M: 09831352950
127	Ekta Incubation Centre	1) Biotechnology 2) IT	West Bengal	Kolkata	AQ 13/1, Sector V, Salt Lake City Kolkata -70000991	http://www.technologyembryo.com/		Mr. Alok Ray, Director, EKTA-TBI info@technologyembryo.com ektaincubationcentre@gmail.com T: (033) 2367 3978

SOURCES

'Digital Marketing Training & Certification Courses: Market Motive'. 2017. *Market Motive.* http://www.marketmotive.com.

Godin, Seth. 2012. *Seth's Blog.* http://sethgodin.typepad.com.

http://www.nature.com/nbt/journal/v21/n2/fig_tab/nbt0203-201_T1.html

IowaInnovationCouncil.http://www.iowainnovationcouncil. com/documents/filelibrary/publication_reports/ IntellectualProperty_AC5C4CEBEC76D.pdf

ipHandbook of Best Practices. http://www.iphandbook.org/ handbook/index.html

Kaushik, Avinash. 2010. 'Search / SEO Metrics & Analytics Questions + Answers'. *Occam's Razor by Avinash Kaushik.* January 20. https://www.kaushik.net/avinash/search-engine-optimization-metrics-analytics-questions-answers/.

Medd, Kerry and Konski, Antoinette. 2003. 'Table 1: A comparison of the four types of intellectual property protection' from article 'Workplace programs to protect trade secrets'. *Nature Biotechnology* 21, 201–03 (2003). doi:10.1038/ nbt0203-201.

Saha, R. 2006. 'Management of Intellectual Property Rights in India'. In *Workshop on IP Management in Public-Private Partnership, Manesar and Bangalore*, 9–35.

World Intellectual Property Organization. http://www.wipo.int/portal/en/index.html

"Blackblot Product Management Professional? (BPMP) Certification Program." *Blackblot - Product Management Expertise?*, www.blackblot.com/certification.

Narayan, Ramkumar. "Product management masterclass.", TiE. Bangalore Aug 2016, Slideshare

General Data Protection Regulation (GDPR). (2020). *General Data Protection Regulation (GDPR) – Official Legal Text*. [online] Available at: https://gdpr-info.eu/ [Accessed 6 Mar. 2020].

GLOSSARY

ADT	Audit
AIDAS	Awareness, Interest, Desire, Action, Satisfaction
ATL	Above the line
B2B	Business to Business
B2C	Business to Consumer
B2B2C	Business to Business to Consumer
BTL	Below the line
CII	Confederation of Indian Industry
CRM	Customer Relationship Management
IIIT-B	Indian Institute of Information Technology, Bangalore
IPR	Intellectual Property Rights
LLP	Limited Liability Partnership
GDPR	General Data Protection Regulation
GPM	Gross Profit Margin
GTM	Go To Market
MBP	Meetings of Board and its powers
M&A	Merger & Acquisition
MVP	Minimum Viable Product
NDA	Non-Disclosure Agreement

ORM	Online Reputation Management
PAN	Permanent Account Number
POSH	Prevention of Sexual Harassment
PR	Public Relations
RSS	Rich Site Summary
SEM	Search Engine Marketing
SM	Service Mark
TDS	Tax Deducted at Source
TM	Trademark
VAT	Value-Added Tax
VC	Venture Capital

FURTHER READING

Horowitz, Ben. The Hard Thing About Hard Things: Building a Business When There Are No Easy Answers. New York: HarperCollins, 2014.

Schmidt, Eric, et al. *Trillion Dollar Coach: The Leadership Handbook of Silicon Valley's Bill Campbell*. Hachette UK, 2019.

Gopalakrishnan, R. *Crash: Lessons from the entry and exit of CEOs*. Penguin Random House India Private, 2018.

'First Round Capital'. 2017. Accessed February 2. http://firstround.com/.

'The Start-up Playbook: Secrets of the Fastest-Growing Start-ups from Their Founding Entrepreneurs'. 2013. *Choice Reviews Online* 50 (11): 50–6284.

'"Give Away Your Legos" and Other Commandments for Scaling Start-ups'. 10 September 2015. http://firstround.com/review/give-away-your-legos-and-other-commandments-for-scaling-start-ups/.

Ast, Clemens H. 2008. 'The Founder's Dilemma'. *Harvard Business Review* 86 (5): 125–125.

Bansal, Rashmi. 2015. *Arise, Awake: The Inspiring Stories of Young Entrepreneurs Who Graduated from College into a Business of Their Own*. Westland.

———. 2014. *Take Me Home: The Inspiring Stories of 20 Entrepreneurs from Small-Town India with Big-Time Dreams*. Westland.

Bossidy, Larry and Charan, Ram. 2008. *Execution: The Discipline of Getting Things Done*. Random House.

Ghoshal, Anupama. 2017. 'The Indian Start-up Ecosystem: Perspectives & Implications'. *Global Journal For Research Analysis* 5 (9). https://worldwidejournals.in/ojs/index.php/gjra/article/view/12200.

Livingston, Jessica. 2008. *Founders at Work: Stories of Start-ups' Early Days*. Apress.

Maurya, Ash. 2012. *Running Lean: Iterate from Plan A to a Plan That Works*. O'Reilly Media, Inc.

———. 2016. *Scaling Lean: Mastering the Key Metrics for Start-up Growth*. Penguin UK.

Mullins, John Walker and Komisar, Randy. 2009. *Getting to Plan B: Breaking Through to a Better Business Model*. Harvard Business Press.

Osterwalder, Alexander and Pigneur, Yves. 2013. *Business Model Generation: A Handbook for Visionaries, Game Changers, and Challengers*. John Wiley & Sons.

Ries, Eric. 2011. *The Lean Start-up: How Constant Innovation Creates Radically Successful Businesses*. Portfolio Penguin.

Ross, Aaron and Tyler, Marylou. 2014. *Predictable Revenue: Turn Your Business Into a Sales Machine with the $100 Million Best Practices of Salesforce.com*. Predictable Revenue, Incorporated.

Soota, Ashok and Gopalan, S.R. 2016. *Entrepreneurship Simplified: From Idea to IPO*. Penguin UK.